Healthy Cooking

HEALTHY HEART COOKBOOK

Healthy Cooking

HEALTHY HEART COOKBOOK

Paul Morgan

AN OCEANA BOOK

This edition published by Silverdale Books,
an imprint of Bookmart Ltd., in 2006

Bookmart Ltd.
Blaby Road
Wigston
Leicester
LE18 4SE

This edition printed 2006

ISBN 1-84509-233-3

QUMHCHH

Manufactured in Singapore by
Pica Digital Pte. Ltd.
Printed in Singapore by
Star Standard Industries (Pte) Ltd

It is always sensible to consult your doctor before changing your diet regime, but it is essential to do so if you suffer from any medical condition or are taking medication of any kind. If you are concerned about any symptoms that develop after changing your diet, consult your doctor immediately. Information is given without any guarantees on the part of the author and publisher, and they cannot be held responsible for the contents of this book.

CONTENTS

INTRODUCTION

For 20 years or more, theories about what constitutes a healthy, heart-friendly diet have chopped and changed. First, all fat was considered to be bad for you – then it was found that some types of fat can protect your heart. Then butter was considered bad, while margarine was thought to be good for you – but after a while, scientists discovered that margarine contained substances called trans fatty acids, which are extremely bad for you. At the same time, all cholesterol was once considered dangerous, but now we know that one type of cholesterol is, in fact, very good for you.

You could be forgiven for being confused. But now, after years of research, scientists have a fairly clear picture of the effect of nutrition on the condition of our heart and blood vessels. There are still some questions to be resolved, however: for example, whether high blood levels of a chemical called homocysteine are a risk factor for heart disease. Nevertheless, the basic facts are now known, and it is beyond question that by avoiding certain foods and eating others you can significantly reduce your chances of developing heart disease and improve your chances of survival if you are already affected by it.

This book will show you how to do just that. First, we will look at what heart disease is and what causes it, and show how the make-up of some foods can cause heart disease while the chemical basis of other foods can prevent it. Then you can choose from a range of mouth-watering, heart-healthy recipes. It may be a cliché, but like many clichés it is true: when it comes to your heart, you really are what you eat!

WHAT IS HEART DISEASE?

During an average lifetime, your heart beats about 2,500 million times. Between 60 and 80 times a minute, at rest, it pumps around 6 litres of life-giving blood through a complex network of arteries and veins.

So what can go wrong? There are problems that we can do little to prevent, such as arrhythmias (abnormal heart rhythms), congenital (occurring before birth) heart defects, cardiomyopathy (a disease of the muscles of the heart) and pericarditis (an infection of the lining around the heart). But the most common problems involve not just the heart but the whole circulatory system, comprising the heart, the arteries and the veins: high blood pressure and atherosclerosis, which can lead not only to a heart attack but also to a stroke and which can, to an extent, be prevented.

A LITTLE OF WHAT YOU FANCY . . .

. . . may not, in fact, do you much good. But, unless your doctor has forbidden it, it is unlikely to do much harm, so long as it is just 'a little' and you do not indulge yourself often. As the recipes in this book show, a healthy diet can be a tasty diet, but, even so, eating completely healthy meals and snacks for seven days a week and 52 weeks a year can be a daunting prospect. So there is no point in worrying if you succumb to the urge to eat a fat-packed doughnut or a greasy hamburger – but only do it from time to time, as a special treat. Try to make sure that at least 90 per cent of your diet is healthy.

Try to get into the habit of eating healthy snacks, for example fruit and nuts, instead of biscuits and crisps.

Pressure points

The phrase 'high blood pressure' means that the force that blood exerts on the walls of arteries as it flows through them is higher than is normal. Blood pressure values are expressed as two figures, representing millimetres of mercury in an old-fashioned blood pressure measuring device (a sphygmomanometer): 120/80, for example, is considered normal – the first figure is the systolic pressure, when the heart is pumping; the second is the diastolic pressure, when the heart is resting between beats. You are considered to have high blood pressure, and will be offered treatment for it, if your reading is 140/90 or higher. It is estimated that between 10 and 20 per cent of the population have high blood pressure, but many people do not know that they have it – there are often no symptoms, which is why it is sometimes known as 'the silent killer'. High blood pressure puts strain on the heart and over time weakens and damages arteries and veins.

Atherosclerosis is the condition in which plaques (atheromata) form on the inner walls of arteries. The plaques consist of dead cells, fibrous tissue and calcium, among other things, but primarily contain cholesterol. They can cause the arteries to harden, narrow and become less flexible (arteriosclerosis), or block them. If atherosclerosis blocks the coronary arteries, which supply the heart with blood, the result will be a heart attack. Sometimes, too, pieces of plaque can break off (thrombi) and be carried around the circulatory system to block other, smaller blood vessels – if these supply blood to the brain, the result could be a stroke.

The nature of the link between atherosclerosis and high blood pressure is complex. Each condition can cause the other one, but generally both develop as a result of lifestyle factors and the natural processes of ageing (some people also have an inherited predisposition to them). Smoking, drinking excessive amounts of alcohol, obesity, high stress levels and the presence of other conditions, such as diabetes, play a major part in the development of both problems, but so, too, does your diet.

The culprits

The main dietary culprits when it comes to developing atherosclerosis and high blood pressure, are saturated fats, trans fats, dietary cholesterol and salt. But some foods can actually prevent both problems. The trick is to know which foods to choose and which to avoid – and what follows will show you.

Choosing olive oil as your main source of dietary fat, combined with eating a healthy diet, can help reduce your risk of cardiovascular disease and diabetes.

KEEP CHECKING

There are often no symptoms if you have high blood pressure – which is why it is known as the silent killer. But it is important that you know what your blood pressure is, so that you can take steps to reduce it if it is too high. In Britain, it is recommended that everybody asks their family doctor to check their blood pressure every five years, and more frequently with age; in the US, the recommendation is that blood pressure should be checked every two years over the age of 20.

You can buy blood pressure monitors for home use, and a wide range of them is available on the internet. However, you should make sure to choose a model whose results have been validated by medical associations, because some models can give inaccurate results.

BLOOD LEVELS

If your blood pressure is too high, a blood sample may be taken so that it can be tested for levels of cholesterol and tryglycerides (the form in which fats are transported in the blood). Depending on the result, you may be advised to adopt healthy eating measures and in some cases may be prescribed statin drugs, which control cholesterol levels.

FATS AND CHOLESTEROL

For many years, scientists believed that the cholesterol that you eat is the villain of the piece when it comes to heart disease. In fact, about 75 per cent of the cholesterol in your blood is manufactured by your liver, while only 25 per cent of it is in your diet. And the liver uses dietary fat to make cholesterol. When this was appreciated, the emphasis moved to eating a low-fat and low-cholesterol diet. But then it was discovered that it is not only the amount of fat in your diet that is important, but how much of which type of fat you eat – and there are three main types of fat: saturated fats, unsaturated fats and trans fats.

Saturated fats are found in meat, poultry, lard and whole-milk dairy products, such as cheese, milk, butter and cream, but high levels are also found in some vegetable oils, such as coconut and palm oil.

Unsaturated fats, which typically are liquid at room temperature, are found in plant and vegetable oils, such as olive, peanut, sesame, safflower, corn, sunflower, canola and soybean oil, and in avocados, oily fish (in the form or omega – 3 fatty acid) and nuts and seeds.

Trans fats are man-made – a by-product of heating vegetable oils in the presence of hydrogen (which is why they are often referred to as 'hydrogenated vegetable oils' on product labels). They are found in commercial baked goods, such as biscuits, snack foods, processed foods and commercially prepared fried foods, such as crisps. Some margarines also contain high levels of trans fats, especially brands that are 'stick' margarines – spreadable ones have less high levels as they are less hydrogenated (hydrogenation makes the fat hard at room temperature).

Where cholesterol comes in

Your body needs cholesterol to function correctly – it is involved in the production of hormones, the body's chemical messengers, as well as bile and vitamin D, and is found in every part of the body. For this reason, it is manufactured in the liver – and the liver uses fats to make it. If you eat too much saturated fat, the liver produces too much cholesterol. And, unfortunately, cholesterol is a soft, waxy substance that can stick to the lining of blood vessels and obstruct them if there are high levels of it in the blood.

As we have seen, liver-produced cholesterol, and so the cholesterol that is ultimately the result of fat consumption, accounts for around 75 per cent of the cholesterol found in your blood. The remaining 25 per cent comes from the cholesterol you eat. Dietary cholesterol is found in eggs, dairy products, meat, poultry, fish and shellfish, but the highest levels are found in egg yolks, meats such as liver and kidneys and shellfish. Vegetables, fruits, nuts, grains, and cereals contain no cholesterol.

'Good' and 'bad' cholesterol

Cholesterol is carried around the body by chemicals called lipoproteins. There are two types: low-density lipoprotein (LDL) and high-density lipoprotein (HDL). If there is too much of the cholesterol carried by LDL, known as ' bad' cholesterol, plaque builds up on arterial walls. But HDL carries cholesterol away from the arteries to the liver, which breaks it down so that it can be excreted from the body; for this reason, HDL cholesterol is said to be 'good' cholesterol.

For some years, scientists have known that saturated fats, and, in particular, trans fats, increase the blood levels of harmful LDL cholesterol and lower levels of beneficial HDL cholesterol, while unsaturated fats have the opposite effect. In January 2005, however, researchers at the Dana-Farber Cancer Institute, in the US, reported that they had discovered the mechanism responsible. It appears that saturated fats trigger a biochemical activator in the liver that boosts LDL cholesterol production.

To sum up, then, a healthy heart diet is one that has low levels of saturated and trans fats, and high levels of unsaturated fats.

FOODS TO USE SPARINGLY
(RICH IN DIETARY CHOLESTEROL)

Organ meats – liver and kidneys

Eggs (especially ones from battery-farmed chickens)

Shellfish

Red meat

FOODS TO CHOOSE

(Containing unsaturated fat)

Vegetable oils – pure olive, peanut, walnut, sesame, corn, soybean, sunflower and safflower oils

Avocados

Oily fish – salmon, mackerel, tuna, herrings and so on

Nuts and seeds

Spreadable, unsaturated margarine

FOODS TO AVOID

(Containing trans fat)

Ready-made commercial foods – cakes, biscuits and snack foods

Processed foods – sausages, pâté, scotch eggs, pies and so on

Commercially prepared fried foods – crisps, battered fish and chips

Hard margarine

FOODS TO USE SPARINGLY

(Containing saturated fat)

Whole-fat milk (skimmed milk is preferable)

Butter, cream, cheese, full-fat yoghurt (low-fat is preferable)

ice cream

Meat – beef, lamb and pork

Poultry – battery-farmed chicken (free-range is preferable), goose, duck and turkey (wild game, such as rabbit, wild duck and venison, is better)

Lard

Eggs (especially ones from battery-farmed chickens)

Coconut oil and *palm oil*

Try to avoid any desserts that have a high level of sugar or saturated fat, for example ice cream.

SALT

The more salt you eat, the more your body retains fluid, and the more fluid there is, the harder your heart has to work to pump blood around your body. And the result of this increase in the heart's work rate is high blood pressure and the risk, over time, of developing heart failure. Some groups of people are said to be 'salt sensitive', and are at particular risk of heart damage even without a rise in blood pressure. They include people with diabetes, the elderly and Afro-Caribbeans.

Doctors recommend that our daily intake of salt should be less than 6 grams – about a teaspoonful. Even less salt than this is recommended for those who already have heart problems. The level is lower for children, too: up to six months old, it is less than 1 gram; between 7 and 12 months it is 1 gram; between 1 and 3 years it is 2 grams; between 4 and 6 it is 3 grams; and between 7 and 10 years it is 5 grams. Worryingly, one small can of spaghetti hoops served on a piece of toast made from white, supermarket bread contains around 0.9 grams – half of a toddler's recommended daily intake.

A FAMILY INHERITANCE

If members of your family suffered heart attacks at an early age – in their 40s or 50s – you may have inherited a condition called hypercholesterolaemia, in which a genetic mutation causes extremely high levels of LDL cholesterol in the blood. It is vital that you consult your doctor if you have such family associations, because if you have inherited the faulty gene you have an 85 per cent chance of suffering a heart attack before the age of 60. You are more likely to suffer from hypercholesterolaemia if you come from one of these populations (in increasing order of likelihood: French Canadians from Quebec; Lebanese Christians; Afrikaners; and Ashkenazi Jews.

It is vital that sufferers adopt strict dietary measures to control their blood cholesterol measures, and statin drugs are often given to help reduce blood levels.

Many people believe that their food will be insipid if they cut down on salt, but this is not true. As an alternative try using herbs, spices, vinegar or lemon juice to add that extra bit of flavour.

Hidden salt

The 6 gram target sounds an easy enough one to achieve, but in fact it is very tall order. The reason is that this target refers to our total salt intake, not just to the salt that we add to our food, and there is a considerable amount of salt hidden in the foods many of us eat. Processed foods are mainly to blame – in fact, researchers estimate that around 75 per cent of our salt intake comes from them.

It is obvious that some foods contain high salt levels: salted nuts, crisps, olives and anchovies, for example, all taste, and are, salty. But bacon, cheese, pickles, stock cubes, sausages and smoked meat and fish contain salt, too. And some brands of biscuits, pizzas, 'ready meals', soups and breakfast cereals are also surprisingly high in salt.

The only way to check which processed foods are high in salt is to read product labels carefully. It is easy to come unstuck when you do this, however, because some labels do not refer to the product's salt content but to its sodium content (salt is made up of sodium and chloride). The two values are not the same – in fact, you have to multiply the sodium value by 2.5 to obtain the real salt content.

Reducing your salt intake

If you cut down on salt, your blood pressure will fall within weeks, even if it was not too high in the first place. And that means that your risk of developing heart disease or having a stroke will also fall.

Many people think that their food will lack taste if they cut down on salt, but this is a myth. You may find that your diet is a little bland for the first week or so, but your taste buds soon adapt. Adopt these salt reduction strategies and you will find the process much more easy.

- **Avoid** processed foods
- **Check** the salt levels of all commercially prepared foods, including everyday products such as bread
- **Throw** away your salt shaker
- **Make** your own salt-free stocks and sauces
- **Use** alternative seasonings, such as lemon juice, herbs and vinegar
- **Eat** fresh fruit (bananas and avocados in particular) and vegetables: the potassium they contain helps counter the effect of dietary salt
- **Do not** switch to sea salt, rock salt or garlic salt – they are not different to normal salt
- **Ask** your doctor whether salt substitutes are suitable for you.

FOODS TO AVOID

All types of salt – table, rock, sea and garlic

Obviously salty foods – anchovies, salted nuts and ready-salted crisps

FOODS TO USE SPARINGLY

(High in salt)

Commercially made foods – biscuits, supermarket bread, cheese biscuits and crisps

Ready-made meals – including pasta, pizzas, curries and Asian cuisine

Tinned foods – baked beans, spaghetti, meats and vegetables

Preserved and smoked foods – bacon, ham, pickles, spiced sausage, stock cubes and sauces

Bananas and avocados are both rich in potassium, which helps counteract the effect of too much salt.

CALCULATE YOUR SALT INTAKE

If you must eat processed foods – and it can be hard not to – try to make sure that you stay within the recommended daily intake of 6 grams of salt. Read a product's label to find the number of grams of salt in 100 grams of the contents. If the quantity of sodium is given, multiply by 2.5 to calculate the actual salt content. (If the value is given in milligrams, or 'mg', divide by 1,000 to convert it to grams.)

Then look for the total weight of the contents, or estimate the proportion of them that you intend to use. Divide the weight that you will use by 100, then multiply by the number of grams of salt in each 100 grams and you will discover how much salt you will eat. The results can be surprising: one small (200g) tin of baked beans can contain as much as 1.7 grams of salt – just under a third of your total recommended intake; one slice of white, refined bread contains 0.61 grams of salt – so just the bread making up a lunchtime sandwich could well account for just under a fifth of your total recommended intake.

SALT SUBSTITUTES

Some people find that their food tastes a little bland when they switch to a low-salt diet, and even though their taste buds will adapt within a few weeks they find that they need a little help to make the change. A number of salt substitutes are on the market, but these contain part sodium and part potassium and in certain circumstances it is possible to overload your body with potassium – consult your doctor before using a commercial salt substitute.

Make your own

This recipe for a salt substitute relies on the principle that a sour flavour is a good substitute for a salty one. It uses the grapefruit peel (or lemon or orange peel, for a weaker taste and citric acid crystal. Also known as 'sour salt' and 'lemon salt', these can be found in the baking section of supermarkets or in delicatessens.

Ingredients *(Makes 3 tablespoons)*

The peel of 1 grapefruit
1 tbsp ground allspice
½ tbsp citric acid crystals

Method

1. Peel the grapefruit as thinly as possible, then scrape away all the white parts. Dry the peel overnight near a source of heat.
2. Grind the dried peel in a coffee grinder or spice grinder, then combine it with the other ingredients. Put the mixture into a well-sealed bottle and shake well to mix. Store in a dry place.

Variation

Add a tablespoon of freshly ground black pepper to the mixture to make it into citrus pepper, an ideal seasoning for meat.

To many people the uses for citrus fruits extend only to drinks and to a few familiar dishes, but in reality their uses are practically limitless.

FOODS TO CHOOSE

('Good' protein – lower in saturated fats)

Vegetables – beans, brown rice, lentils, millet and pulses

Soybeans

Nuts – brazil, peanuts and pinenuts

Seeds – sesame

Free-range chicken and turkey (but remove the skin)

Locally sourced lean cuts of non-intensively reared meats – beef, lamb, pork and veal

Free-range chicken eggs (but not duck or goose eggs)

PROTEIN

Protein, made up from chemicals called amino acids, makes up the building blocks of all our body's tissues except stored fat. You need to eat a certain amount of protein every day – a minimum of one gram for every kilogram of body weight – to prevent the body from starting to break down tissue. And you need more than that if you want to build up healthy muscles and bones.

It is easy to get enough protein in your diet in Western industrialised societies, though hard to do so in developing countries. But the quantity of protein you eat is not the whole story. What is important is that you eat a variety of amino acids, which means protein from a variety of sources. This does not mean that it is essential to eat steaks, for example, because you can obtain a full range of proteins from vegetable and fruit sources, if you are a vegetarian. Variety is the watchword.

Protective protein?

Scientists have theorised that eating large amounts of protein might have beneficial effects on the cardiovascular system, but the question has not yet been resolved. However, one large-scale, 14-year study – the Nurses' Health Study, in the US – showed that women who ate about 110 grams of protein a day were 25 per cent less likely to suffer from heart problems than women who ate 68 grams a day; whether the protein came from animal or vegetable sources did not matter, and nor did the fat levels in the women's diet. So there are certainly no dangers to eating relatively large amounts of protein, though preferably from sources that do not contain saturated fats, and there may be a beneficial effect.

One protein that has definitively been shown to help prevent heart disease by lowering cholesterol levels is soy. An analysis of 38 different trials has shown that eating 50 grams of soy protein a day instead of animal protein lowered LDL cholesterol levels by 12.9 per cent – a significant figure. Some newspaper reports have suggested that soy may have a feminizing effect, because soybeans are rich in chemicals called phytooestrogens (related to the female hormone, oestrogen). However, research studies have found that this is not the case.

Besides tasting so good, nuts are an excellent source of protein as well as the B vitamins, vitamin E and minerals such as iron, calcium, magnesium and potassium.

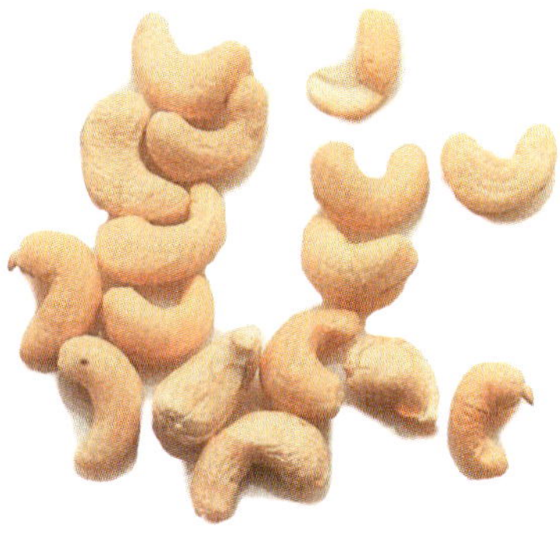

CARBOHYDRATES

Carbohydrates are the body's primary source of fuel and are an essential part of a healthy diet. There are three types of carbohydrate: sugars, fibre and starch, and all of them are built from molecules of sugar. They used to be described as 'complex' or 'simple' carbohydrates, depending on whether they were simple forms of sugar or consisted of linked forms of sugar, and it was believed that simple carbohydrates should be avoided and complex ones preferred.

CHECK THE LABEL

Food labels can be misleading, so it is important to read them carefully. Phrases such as 'made with wheat flour' do not necessarily mean that the product is a whole-grain food. To be sure that it is, look for a main ingredient that is specifically described as being 'whole-grain'.

The glycaemic index

Today this categorization is now longer used. Instead, nutritionists classify carbohydrates according to their glycaemic index. During the digestive process, carbohydrates are broken down into the simplest forms of sugar, and the glycaemic index (GI) measures how quickly this happens and so how fast levels of sugar in the blood rise – a high glycaemic index value means that the carbohydrate raises these levels very quickly.

The significance of this is that the pancreas starts to produce the hormone insulin in response to rising blood sugar levels, which promotes the uptake of sugar by the body's cells and reduces sugar levels in the blood. If you continually eat foods with a high glycaemic index – and if you have a hereditary disposition to the problem or are overweight and inactive – the levels of both insulin and sugar in your blood remain high, and you develop what is known as insulin resistance. This can not only lead to type 2 diabetes, but result in high blood pressure, low levels of 'good' cholesterol and the risk of heart disease.

High or low?

In essence, whether a food has a high or low glycaemic index depends on how quickly its carbohydrates are converted to simple sugar during the digestive process. Foods that have not been processed – whole-grain foods – still contain their original fibre, which slows down the rate at which carbohydrates are converted to simple sugars and so also slows down the rate at which sugar enters the bloodstream. However, the type of starch in the food is important, too: potatoes, for example, contain a starch that is broken down quickly during digestion. Other factors affecting the GI value are: ripeness – ripe fruit has a higher GI than unripe fruit; acidity – vinegar and lemon juice delay stomach emptying and so reduce the GI value; and the size of food particles – small particles are more easily absorbed and increase the GI value.

Low GI foods include soy, beans, fruit, milk and grainy bread; medium ones include sugar, orange juice and oats; while high GI foods include potatoes, rice, and wholemeal and white bread. It might seem a daunting prospect to exist solely on low GI foods, but it is not necessary to do so. Luckily, however, eating a low GI food reduces the GI value of high GI foods when they are eaten at the same time – if you eat cornflakes (high GI) with milk (low GI) your blood sugar levels will not go up as quickly – what is known as the 'glycaemic load' is reduced. So if you plan your menus carefully you can still eat some high GI foods.

It is hard to think of any other common, widely used foodstuff that provides as many benefits as the soya bean. The nutritional advantages that soy can provide are numerous. It is the most complete form of high-quality vegetable protein available, and is high in essential amino acids, especially lysine, which makes it very similar to animal proteins such as meat and eggs.

FOODS TO CHOOSE

(Low glycaemic index carbohydrates)

Bran and porridge oats

Barley, buckwheat and bulgar wheat

Some fruits – apples, citrus, berries, peaches, pears, plums and rhubarb

Pasta

Some vegetables – avocados, aubergines, beans (runner and green), broccoli, cabbage, cauliflower, carrots, celery, courgettes, cucumber, leeks, onions, lettuce, mushrooms, olives, peas, peppers, spinach and tomatoes

FOODS TO USE SPARINGLY

(Medium glycaemic index carbohydrates)

Pure wheat cereals

Granary and whole-wheat bread

Basmati or long-grained rice, wild rice and couscous

Corn – cornmeal, corn oil, sweetcorn

Some fruit – apricots, bananas, melon, dried fruit, pineapples and mangoes

Vegetables – new potatoes, sweet potatoes, beetroot and artichokes

Honey

FOODS TO AVOID

(High glycaemic index carbohydrates)

Breakfast cereals – cornflakes and sugar-coated cereals

White bread, cakes, biscuits, bagels, buns, muffins, pancakes and doughnuts

White and brown rice

Some fruits – dates, prunes and watermelon

Gnocchi

Some vegetables – broad beans, potatoes (when mashed, baked, fried or roasted), parsnips and swede

Sugar – table, glucose, treacle and molasses

Tomato ketchup

THE DANGERS OF BEING OVERWEIGHT

Being overweight brings with it the dangers of many health problems, but if you carry the extra pounds on your waist – in the classic 'beer belly'—you are far more at risk of developing heart disease or diabetes. In fact, men with waists of more than 101 cm (40 in) and women with waists of more than 89cm 35 in are at between double and quadruple the risk of developing them. The reason is that fat that is stored around the stomach secretes hormones that play havoc with the production of insulin, the pancreatic hormone that controls blood sugar levels. As a result 'insulin resistance' develops, leading to diabetes, high blood pressure and high cholesterol levels.

For those people who follow a healthy diet, fresh summer fruits are most certainly considered nutrient-rich foods. There are many things inside fresh fruits and vegetables that make them highly beneficial. They provide an array of vitamins, potassium and dietary fibre in addition to important phytonutrients that are thought to protect against cancer, heart disease and other diseases associated with ageing.

FIBRE

Our bodies cannot digest some of the food that we eat, and it is this indigestible material that is known as dietary fibre. Most people know that a diet high in fibre is good for your bowel function and can protect against disorders of the intestines, such as cancer of the colon, but it is less well known that fibre can also lower the levels of cholesterol in your blood.

There are two types of fibre: insoluble and soluble (the latter is so-called because it forms a gel when mixed with liquid). Insoluble fibre plays the main part in promoting bowel function, and high levels of it are found in foods such as whole-wheat bread, wheat cereals, rice, barley, grains, cabbage, carrots and so on. But it is soluble fibre that reduces blood cholesterol – though it is not clear how it does this. It is found in oats, oat bran, oatmeal, peas, beans, barley and fruits.

Five a day

So it makes sense to increase your intake of foods rich in fibre, and especially of those rich in soluble fibre – generally, it is recommended that you should eat five portions of fibre-rich fruit and vegetables a day. And, of course, foods such as these are low in saturated fats and cholesterol. Make sure that you read labels carefully, though, because some commercial products that claim to be rich in fibre in fact contain very little of it.

FOODS TO CHOOSE

(High in soluble fibre)

Oatmeal and oat bran

Lentils, beans and peas

Apples, bananas, blueberries, oranges, pears and strawberries

Sweetcorn, spinach, spring greens and broccoli

Nuts – almonds, brazil, hazel, peanuts, pecan, pistachio and walnuts

Seeds – sesame, sunflower and pumpkin

FOODS TO USE

(High in insoluble fibre)

Whole grains – bran, wheat, couscous, brown rice, bulgur and barley

Whole-wheat and granary bread

Whole-wheat pasta

Whole-wheat flour

Wholegrain breakfast cereals

Fruit – both fresh and dried

All vegetables – but especially brussel sprouts, carrots, cabbage, okra, parsnips, sweetcorn, courgettes, cucumber, celery, tomatoes and unpeeled potatoes

Whole-wheat bread or rolls are high in insoluble fibre. This type of fibre creates a feeling of fullness in the stomach, and its water-holding quality helps to create bulk and moisture in the bowels.

VITAMINS, MINERALS AND ANTIOXIDANTS

There is absolutely no doubt that every one of our body's systems need vitamins and minerals to function, and the cardiovascular system is no exception. Vitamins act as catalysts, initiating and controlling chemical reactions in the body. Only small amounts of them are needed – they are known as micronutrients – and they must be obtained from our diet, because the body cannot manufacture them. If you follow the rules for healthy eating given in this book, and take a multivitamin supplement every day, as a precaution, you should absorb all the vitamins and minerals that your body requires. But sometimes the way that we treat and cook food reduces its content of micronutrients. Follow these rules to make sure that you can meet your body's requirements.

- Avoid processed foods, and canned foods in particular, because these can be low in vitamin content.

- Always use fresh or frozen fruit and vegetables, because vitamin levels decrease as these foods age. It is not generally realised that freezing preserves vitamin content, but chilling fruit and vegetables in a refrigerator before heating them can reduce levels of vitamins such as vitamin C and folic acid by up to 30 per cent. Remember that frozen vegetables – peas, especially – are often more vitamin-rich than fresh ones, because they are frozen immediately after being picked.

- Keep all foods away from heat, light and air, all of which reduce levels of vitamin C and the B vitamins. Store vegetables in airtight bags.

- Use the skin of fruits and vegetables wherever possible and avoid trimming them too much. Instead of peeling, wash or scrub the – most of the nutritional value of fruits and vegetables is contained in the skin or the area underneath it.

- Keep the water you have used to cook vegetables and use it as a base for stock or sauces – otherwise you will lose the valuable vitamins and minerals that have leached into the water.

Use the skin of fruit and vegetables where possible – instead of peeling, wash and scrub them.

- Take a daily multivitamin supplement – it can be hard to obtain sufficient quantities of some vitamins, such as B12 and folic acid, from your diet; and fibre-rich foods contain chemicals called phytates, which can bind with some minerals and interfere with their absorption. But think of it as a nutritional safety net, rather than as a substitute for healthy eating.

Homocysteine

Some research has linked high levels of a protein called homocysteine in the blood with high levels of the 'bad', plaque-causing LDL cholesterol, which raises blood pressure. The theory is that homocysteine changes cholesterol into this 'bad' form. Normally, homocysteine is broken down to form new proteins for the body with the help of vitamins B6 and B12 and folic acid, and it is thought that people with high homocysteine levels may lack sufficient of these vitamins in their diet.

Research has yet to confirm this theory, though several studies are ongoing and more should be known soon. Until the results are in, however, it would be sensible to make sure that you eat sufficient vitamin B6 and B12 and folic acid in your diet. Foods rich in them include asparagus, avocados, bananas, beans, cabbage, carrots, fish, lentils and spinach, and – though these should be eaten sparingly – cheese, milk, beef, yoghurt and eggs.

Antioxidants

Many of our bodily structures can be damaged by the presence of what are known as 'free radicals'—technically speaking, these are atoms that have unpaired electrons. The most common free radical is radical oxygen, which can damage cells and increase the likelihood that LDL 'bad' cholesterol forms fatty plaques in arteries, leading to heart disease.

When this was realised, in the 1990s, nutritionists started to look at the antioxidants, which combat radical oxygen – the most common ones being vitamins C and E and beta-carotene (a precursor to vitamin A) and lycopene. Soon antioxidant supplements became increasingly popular, and today some 30 per cent of Americans take them. Unfortunately, they do not reduce the risks of heart disease or stroke, as a series of studies, and meta-studies (that is, studies of studies), have shown.

Nevertheless, it has been shown that a diet that is high in antioxidants is protective against heart disease. The answer to this conundrum is thought to be that in practice the effect of dietary antioxidant relies on the interaction between the antioxidants and other dietary ingredients: minerals, perhaps, or fibre. So it is important to eat a diet rich in antioxidants – that means richly coloured fruit and vegetables that contain chemicals called flavonoids, such as apricots, blueberries, bilberries, broccoli, carrots, mangos, peppers and spinach, and, in particular, tomatoes (though these should be cooked to release maximum quantities of flavonoids). And, just to show that a healthy heart diet need not be without its luxuries, there are high levels of flavonoids in both dark chocolate and red wine – though both should be enjoyed in moderation.

A fresh vegetable salad is far more beneficial in terms of nutritic value than cooked vegetables. Try to find ways to enjoy fresh flavours of vegetables in an assortment of recipes.

TOO MUCH CAN BE DANGEROUS

Many people take high doses of vitamin supplements, without having taken medical advice. But doing so can be dangerous, because in many cases the effects of high doses are not known, and in some cases the effects have been confirmed to be dangerous. For example, it was once thought that vitamin E in very high doses might help prevent heart disease, but several studies have failed to show this and a recent study suggests that they may make heart failure more likely. And the list goes on: too much calcium can lead to lethargy, confusion and coma; excess vitamin B6 can cause a nerve disorder that leads to loss of feeling in the arms and legs; high doses of vitamin A can increase the risk of cardiovascular disease and can damage your liver; excessive doses of vitamin C can cause abdominal pain, nausea and diarrhoea; and so on.

The message is clear: do not take high-dose vitamin supplements unless they have been prescribed by your doctor – you can obtain all the vitamins and minerals you need by eating a healthy diet and taking a daily multivitamin supplement.

VITAMIN- AND MINERAL-RICH FOODS

(NB Pre-menopausal women and women taking HRT should eat more of foods containing vitamins that are depleted by the female hormone oestrogen.)

Vitamin A (antioxidant)
Retinol: butter, cod liver oil, cheese and Beta-carotene: apricots, cantaloupe, carrots, kale, peach, peas, spinach and sweet potatoes.

Vitamin B1
Beans, brown rice, milk, oatmeal, vegetables, whole grains and yeast (depleted by alcohol, caffeine, exposure to air and water, food additives and oestrogen).

Vitamin B2
Eggs, fish, meat, milk, vegetables and whole grains (depleted by alcohol, caffeine, oestrogen and zinc).

Vitamin B3
Avocado, eggs, fish, meat, peanuts, prunes, seeds and whole grains (destroyed by canning and some sleeping pills; depleted by alcohol and oestrogen).

Vitamin B5
Bran, eggs, green vegetables, meat, whole grains and yeast (destroyed by canning).

Vitamin B6
Avocado, bananas, cabbage, cantaloupe, fish, milk, eggs, seeds and wheat bran (destroyed by alcohol, heat, oestrogen and processing techniques during production of commercial food).

Vitamin B folic acid
Apricots, avocados, beans, carrots, green vegetables, melons, oranges and whole wheat (destroyed by commercial food processing techniques, cooking and exposure to water and air, depleted by alcohol).

Vitamin B12
Dairy products, fish and meat (depleted by alcohol, exposure to sunlight and water, oestrogen and sleeping tablets).

Vitamin C (antioxidant)
Broccoli, cabbage, cauliflower, citrus fruits, green peppers, spinach, tomatoes and potatoes (destroyed by boiling, exposure to air and carbon dioxide and long storage; depleted by alcohol, aspirin, oestrogen, stress and tobacco).

Vitamin D
Cod liver oil, dairy products and oily fish. (depleted by lack of sunlight).

Vitamin E (antioxidant)
Almonds, broccoli, eggs, kale, oats, olive oil, peanuts, soybeans, seeds, spinach and wheat germ (destroyed by commercial food processing techniques, freezing, heat, oxygen and chlorine; depleted by smoking and use of contraceptive pills).

Vitamin K
Broccoli, cod liver oil, eggs, green vegetables, live yoghurt, tomatoes and whole grains.

Magnesium
Bitter chocolate, brown rice, nuts, soybeans and whole wheat (depleted by caffeine and stress).

Zinc (antioxidant)
Eggs, meat, mushrooms, yeast and whole grains (inhibited by caffeine and smoking).

Potassium
Avocados, bananas, dried fruit, green vegetables, nuts and potatoes.
(lost in diarrhoea and sweat).

Selenium (antioxidant)
Broccoli, onions, tomatoes, tuna and wheat germ.

STRIKING A BALANCE

It is easy to decide which foods you should eat, but more difficult to decide how often to eat them. It is also hard to strike a nutritional balance between foods so that you obtain all the nutrients that your body demands in the correct quantities, yet protect your heart and arteries at the same time. And you will have noticed already from the tables in this book that certain foods are 'good' in the sense that they contain substantial quantities of a desirable ingredient, but 'not so good' in that they contain less desirable ingredients. So how do you do it?

The healthy eating pyramid shown on the opposite indicates how often you should eat the different food groups. For instance, while foods such as cheese and other dairy products are important as part of a balanced diet, you should try to use these sparingly because of the high levels of saturated fat they contain.

Combined with exercise, a balanced diet low in saturated fat is essential in achieving a healthy heart. All the recipes in this book are specifically designed to help you with this, and they show that a healthy diet can be full of variety and flavour.

EXPLAINING THE SYMBOLS

SOLUBLE FIBRE

HIGH
MEDIUM
LOW

PROTEIN

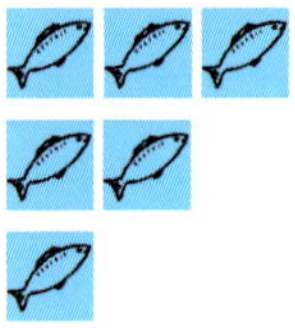

HIGH
MEDIUM
LOW

ANTIOXIDANT

HIGH
MEDIUM
LOW

SATURATED FAT

HIGH
MEDIUM
LOW

UNSATURATED FAT

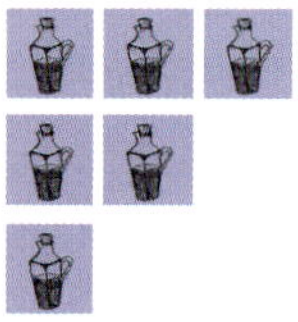

HIGH
MEDIUM
LOW

CHOLESTEROL

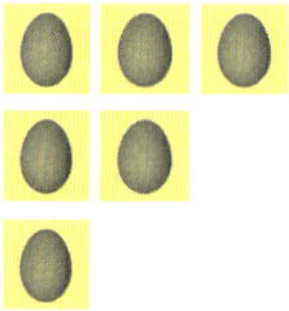

HIGH
MEDIUM
LOW

GLYCAEMIC INDEX

HIGH
MEDIUM
LOW

INSOLUBLE FIBRE

HIGH
MEDIUM
LOW

HEALTHY EATING PYRAMID

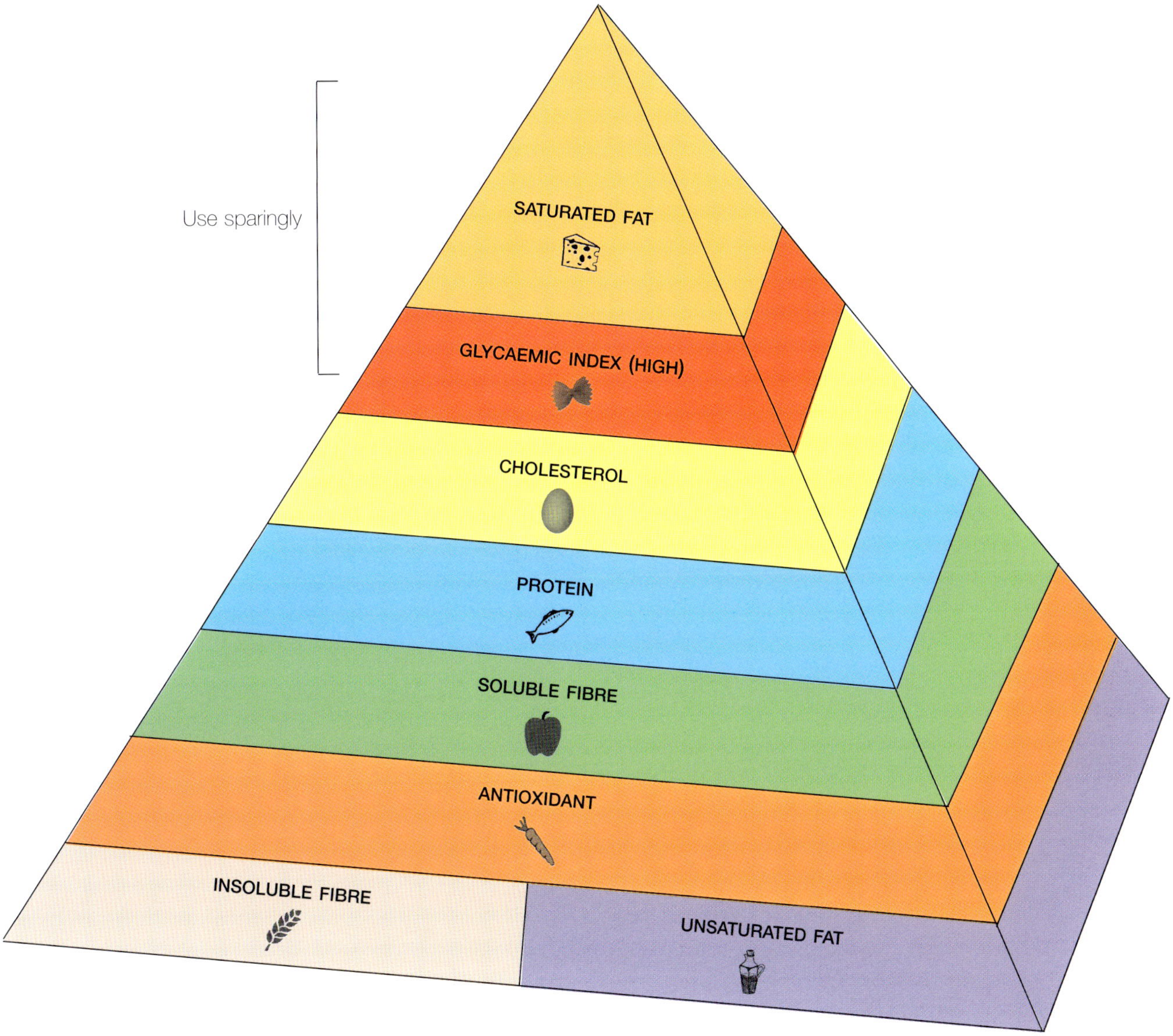

Saturated Fat: Red meat, goose, duck, cheese, butter, cream, full-fat yogurt

Glycaemic Index (HIGH): Rice, white bread, potatoes, desserts, broad beans, prunes, watermelon, and pasta

Cholesterol: Eggs, butter, cream, cheese, shellfish, pork, lamb, beef (0–1 times daily)

Protein: Fish, shellfish, free-range chicken, rabbit, wild game, low-fat dairy (1–2 times daily)

Soluble Fibre: Oats, barley, peas, beans, fruits (e.g. apples, oranges, bananas, walnuts) nuts (2–3 times daily)

Antioxidant: Spinach, broccoli, garlic, onions, red and orange vegetables and fruit, berries (at most meals)

Insoluble Fibre: Wheat bran, whole-wheat flour, wild rice, grains, cabbage, cauliflower, fruit skins (at most meals)

Unsaturated Fat: Olive oil, soya beans, avocado, peanuts, salmon, mackerel, tuna, sardines (1–2 times daily)

HOW TO COOK HEALTHILY

There is little point in choosing healthy heart ingredients and recipes if you cook them in a way that is in itself unhealthy. It is important to choose cooking methods that not only help reduce cholesterol and saturated fats and keep the calorie count low, but maximise the nutritional value of each dish. These techniques are effective, but may require a little practice:

- Baking – good for vegetables, fruit, poultry and lean meat, as well as for puddings; you may need a little extra liquid
- Braising or stewing – brown first, on top of the stove, then cook in a small quantity of liquid; if you leave the dish in a refrigerator you can remove the chilled fat and then reheat it
- Grilling – on a rack, so that fat can drain away
- Microwaving – place the food between two paper towels to drain fat away while it cooks
- Poaching – in a covered pan of the correct size, so that you use the minimum liquid
- Roasting – on a rack so that the food does not sit in fat; baste with fat-free liquids, such as wine or lemon juice
- Sautéing – use a high heat and a small amount of non-stick cooking spray, or just cook without spray if you have a good-quality non-stick pan
- Steaming – in a perforated basket over simmering water; add seasoning to the water for extra flavour
- Stir-frying – in a wok, using a small amount of non-stick cooking spray or a tiny amount of olive oil.

You can also increase flavour, reduce fat and salt content and make the most of your ingredients' nutritional value if you

REMEMBER TO:

- Check labels for common ingredients, such as soy sauce, baking soda and monosodium glutamate – these all contain high levels of sodium and should be used very sparingly, if at all
- Make your own stock rather than using pre-prepared cubes, which can be high in salt
- Steam vegetables, for preference, in order to maximise both their flavour and nutritional value
- Cook lightly to preserve vitamin content (but cook meats and other foods that may harbour disease-producing organisms thoroughly)
- Choose extra virgin olive oil and vinegar rather than salted, pre-prepared salad dressings
- Wash canned vegetables before use – by doing so you can substantially reduce their salt content
- Use only one egg yolk when making scrambled eggs or omelettes, but mix in two or three extra egg whites
- Trim as much fat as you can from meat before you cook it and remove the skin from poultry
- Choose lean, low-fat meats, such as game (but, again, remember to remove the skin) and venison
- Drain oil from canned fish and rinse the fish in water before you use it
- Use herbs, lemon juice, wine and freshly ground pepper to enhance flavours.

Use fresh herbs (l-r flat-leaf parsley, rosemary, basil and dill) to flavour your sauces rather than salt.

MAKE YOUR OWN STOCK

Many stock cubes contain high levels of salt and low levels of nutrients. But nothing could be more simple than making your own stock, and if you make it in large batches you can freeze it for later use. You can use your stock as the basis for a delicious soup – serve it with a whole-grain roll – or as the basis of a nourishing stew or a piquant sauce.

FISH STOCK

Ingredients

1 kg fish bones, heads (with gills removed) and tails (sole or plaice are tastiest, but any other white, non-oily fish will do)
1 large onion, coarsely chopped
2 shallots, coarsely chopped
2 ribs of celery, tops included, coarsely chopped
2 large carrots, scrubbed but not peeled, coarsely chopped
2 bay leaves
2 cloves
6 sprigs of parsley, coarsely chopped
1 tbsp peppercorns
Lemon rind from half a lemon
Cold water to cover

Method

Place everything in a stockpot and bring to simmering point – do not allow to boil. Simmer for 20–30 minutes, but no longer or the stock will become bitter. Strain through cheesecloth or use a non-metallic colander. Reduce the strained stock by boiling, if required. Use or freeze as required.

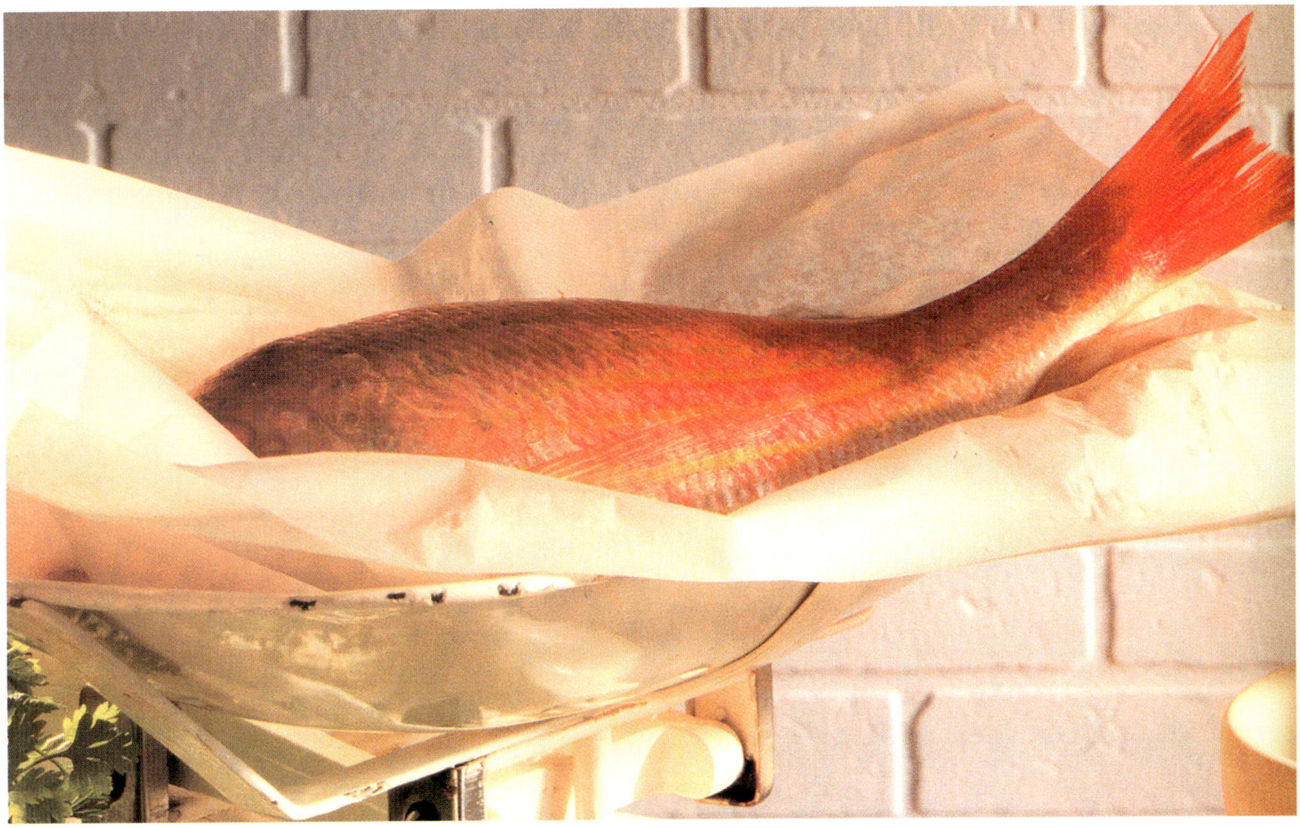

Salt-water fish are a superior source of nutrients, which are vital to growth and good health. Fish yield high amounts of proteins, vitamins, minerals and unsaturated fats.

VEGETABLE STOCK

Ingredients

3 large carrots, scrubbed but not peeled, coarsely chopped
1 turnip, coarsely chopped
2 onions, coarsely chopped
2 leeks, coarsely chopped
4 ribs of celery, including tops, coarsely chopped
Coarsely chopped trimmings from cauliflower, spinach, broccoli or any other vegetables, so long as they are fresh and clean. Always use fresh vegetables.
1 cup any dried beans, having been soaked overnight, if necessary; or use rice or barley
2 tbsp olive oil
1 bouquet garni, which includes 3 sprigs parsley, 1 sprig thyme and 1 bay leaf
1 tbsp peppercorns
Approx 3 litres cold water for 1 kg vegetables

Method

Warm the olive oil in a stockpot, add the vegetables and simmer, stirring continuously for 15 minutes until they start to colour slightly. Then add the water and the other ingredients and bring to simmering point. Simmer for at least 2 hours, adding more water if necessary. Then strain through cheesecloth or use a non-metallic colander. Use or freeze, as required.

CHICKEN STOCK

Ingredients

The bones of a chicken, and, if available, a ham bone or a veal knuckle (ask your butcher for one)
2 leeks, coarsely chopped
2 large carrots, scrubbed but not peeled, coarsely chopped
3 large onions, coarsely chopped
2 ribs of celery, tops included, coarsely chopped
6 sprigs of parsley, coarsely chopped
1 large clove of garlic
2 cloves
1 tbsp peppercorns
Lemon rind from half a lemon

Method

Place the bones in a stockpot and cover with cold water. Bring to simmering point – do not allow to boil. Simmer for at least an hour, then add all other ingredients and more cold water to cover, if necessary. Return to simmering point and simmer for another 2 hours. Then strain through cheesecloth or use a non-metallic colander. Refrigerate, and when stock has set remove any fat from the top. Use or freeze, as required.

Use the chicken stock for the basis of soups and stews.

There is evidence to suggest that two units of alcohol, especially red wine, can help reduce blood pressure. Pictured here are grapes grown in Geneva, which make a rich fruity wine.

THE HEALTHY HEART LIFESTYLE

Eating heart-friendly dishes is only one part of the healthy heart lifestyle. To reduce blood pressure, lower cholesterol levels and promote cardiovascular health, you should also:

Give up smoking – if you smoke, you have more than double the risk of having a heart attack than a non-smoker, and you are more likely not to survive a heart attack

Manage stress – use relaxation techniques and anger-management methods to cope with stress and keep your blood pressure low

Lose weight – if you are overweight, you are between two and six times more likely to develop high blood pressure; but resist the temptation to go on a crash diet, because permanent weight loss is only achieved by reducing your calorific input and increasing the amount of exercise you do in the long term: aim to lose between a pound and half-a-pound a week

Cut down on alcohol – there is evidence to suggest that two units of alcohol, and especially of red wine, can reduce blood pressure, but more than this can increase blood pressure

Lead an active life – even small amounts of physical activity, for example walking or gardening, can reduce the risk of developing heart disease.

TABLES

These tables give the nutritional values for the main ingredients used in the recipes that follow. To eat healthily and minimise your risk of developing heart disease, the major part of your diet should consist of foods with a low fat content, a medium or, better, low glycaemic index, moderate protein levels and a high fibre content. Use the Healthy Eating Pyramid on page 21 as a guide to proportions.

Remember that carrying excess weight is a major risk for developing heart problems, and watch your calorie intake, too. Doctors recommend that men with a sedentary lifestyle – that of an office worker, say – should eat 2,700 calories a day, while women should eat 2,000. In order to lose weight gradually, at the rate of a pound a week, you need to reduce this figure by 500 calories.

Food	Quantity	Fat	Glycaemic index	Protein	Fibre	Calories
Meat and Dairy						
Cheese, feta	20 g	6	M	4	0	80
Cheese, reduced fat	20 g	4.5	M	7	0	70
Chicken skinless	100 g	5	L	30	0	150
Crème fraîche, low fat	100 ml	17.5	M	3	0	800
Egg	1 medium	5.5	M	6	0	80
Lean beef, lamb, pork	100 g	7	M	30	0	190
Milk, low fat	250 ml	2.5	L	8	0	102
Rabbit	100 g	4.5	L	30	0	160
Wild fowl	100 g	6	L	30	0	155
Yoghurt	100 ml	0	L	5	0	40
Fish						
Herring, salmon	100 g	11	L	20	0	180
Mackerel	100 g	18	L	25	0	220
Sardine	100 g	2	L	15	0	65
Shellfish	100 g	1	L	15	0	105
Trout	100 g	6	L	20	0	155
Tuna	100 g	3	L	20	0	120
White fish	100 g	2	L	20	0	90

Prawns are an excellent low-calorie choice on the food chain, and they are a rich source of protein, vitamins and minerals.

Food	Quantity	Fat	Glycaemic index	Protein	Fibre	Calories
Fruit						
Apple	1 medium	0	L	0.5	2	45
Apricot	3	0	M	1.5	2	30
Banana	1 small	0.5	M	1	1	90
Berries, fresh	100 g	0	L	0.5	1	30
Dried fruit	50 g	0	M	0.5	4	80
Grapefruit	half	0	L	0.5	1	30
Melon	slice	0	M	0.5	1	50
Nectarine, peach	1 medium	0	L	0.5	1	35
Orange	1 medium	0	L	1.5	3	50

Fruit is easily digested and exercises a cleansing effect on the blood and the digestive tract.

Food	Quantity	Fat	Glycaemic index	Protein	Fibre	Calories
Vegetables						
Aubergine	100 g	0	L	0.5	2	75
Avocado	½ medium	15	L	2	3.5	150
Beans	100 g	0.5	L	6	4	100
Beetroot	small	0	L	0.5	0.5	25
Broccoli	100 g	0	L	1.5	2.5	25
Cabbage	50 g	0	L	1	1	7
Carrot	50 g	0	L	0.5	1	12

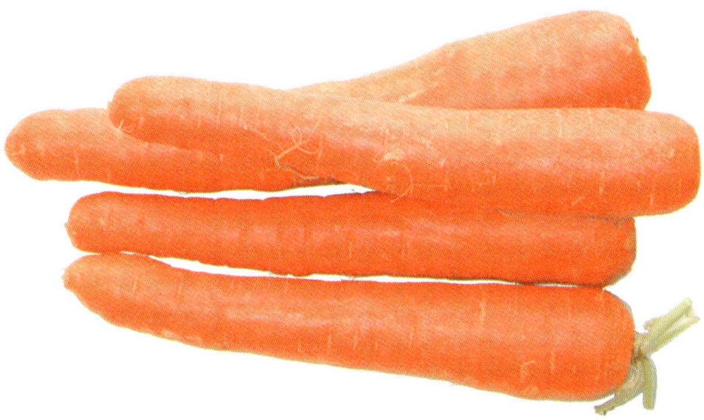

Carrots are eaten mainly for the beta-carotene (providing vitamin A value) and cooking carrots actually enhances the digestibility of the beta-carotene.

Food	Quantity	Fat	Glycaemic index	Protein	Fibre	Calories
Vegetables *(continued)*						
Cauliflower	50 g	0	L	1	1.5	20
Green beans	100 g	0	L	1.5	2.5	20
Onions	medium	0	L	1	1.4	30
Peas	100 g	0	L	3.5	6	60
Peppers	100 g	0	L	1	2.5	30
Potatoes, new	3	0	M	1.5	3	100
Soyabean	100 g	7	L	8	6	120
Spinach	50 g cooked	0	L	1	1	10
Squash, butternut	100 g	0	M	1	1.5	30
Sweetcorn	100 g	0. 5	M	2.5	1.5	95
Tofu	100 g	4	L	8	0	70
Tomato	medium	0	L	1	1	15

Eating raw onions can help to reduce cholesterol levels because they increase levels of high-density lipoproteins. Onions can also help in preventing coronary heart disease, thrombosis and blood pressure.

Peppers are low in calories and are especially rich in vitamins A and C. Surprisingly, peppers contain three to four times more vitamin C than an orange. They do not contain any fat and help to stimulate the circulation.

Food	Quantity	Fat	Glycaemic index	Protein	Fibre	Calories
Cereal, Nuts, Pulses						
Barley	50 g raw	1	L	2	1	140
Chickpeas	100 g	3	L	5	4	110
Lentils	100 g	0.5	L	8	2	100
Oats	50 g raw	1	L	4	3	140
Pasta, wholegrain	100 g	1	L	5	4	120
Rice, brown, basmati	100 g	0	M	3.5	1	200
Walnuts	2 tbsp	8	L	2	1	80
Wild rice	100 g	0	M	3	1	100

BREAKFASTS

HUNGARIAN OAT PANCAKES

SERVES **4**

Oat pancakes, like any others, freeze well, so it is a good idea to make a double batch and store them.

50 g rolled porridge oats
50 g wholewheat flour
1 tsp grated orange rind
150 ml orange juice
150 ml skimmed milk
2 egg whites, lightly beaten
oil, for brushing
2 tbsp light muscovado sugar

FILLING

225 g low-fat cottage cheese
175 g seedless raisins
1 tsp grated orange rind

GARNISH

orange segments

1 In a bowl, mix together the oats, flour and orange rind. Gradually pour on the orange juice and milk, beating constantly. Fold in the egg whites. Lightly brush a non-stick omelette pan with oil and heat it over medium heat. Pour in just enough of the batter to cover the base, and tip the pan to spread it evenly. Cook the pancake until it bubbles and is browned on the underside. Flip or toss it and cook on the other side.

NUTRITIONAL VALUES

2 Cook the remainder of the batter in the same way. Depending on the size of the pan, the mixture should make 8–10 pancakes.

3 Mix together the cheese, raisins and orange rind for the filling. Spread about 3 tablespoons of the mixture in the centre of each pancake and roll them up. You can prepare the pancakes to this stage, cover and store in the refrigerator overnight.

4 Set the grill to medium. Arrange the pancakes in a flameproof dish and sprinkle them with the sugar. Grill until the sugar caramelizes then serve hot, decorated with the orange segments.

BREAKFAST CRUNCH

SERVES **4**

Packed with flavour and full of vitamins, this breakfast cereal can be partly made up in advance to save time in the mornings. Roast the seeds and pine kernels, and store them in airtight containers ready for use.

25 g sunflower seeds

25 g pine kernels

25 g sesame seeds

2 oranges

2 tbsp brown sugar

50 g dried figs, chopped

2 large bananas

600 ml low-fat Greek yoghurt

NUTRITIONAL VALUES

1. Using a dry frying pan, roast the sunflower seeds and pine nuts for 3 minutes over a moderate heat. Add the sesame seeds and roast for a further 3 minutes, stirring to give an even browning. Remove the pan from the heat and leave to cool.

2. Coarsely grate the rind from 1 orange and add to the pan with the sugar and dried figs. Stir until thoroughly combined and cook for 2 minutes. Leave to cool.

3. Remove the rind and pith from the oranges and cut them into pieces. Slice the bananas and mix the oranges and yoghurt. Divide among four dishes and top each with the fig mixture. Serve at once.

GRAPEFRUIT COCKTAILS

SERVES **4**

As with other citrus fruit, grapefruit is believed to slow down the rate of sugar metabolism. Here the fruit is transformed into a refreshing cocktail to start the day.

2 large juicy grapefruit

Peel the grapefruit and remove all the pith. Hold the fruit over a bowl and use a sharp serrated knife to cut in toward the middle of the fruit, removing the fleshy segments and leaving behind the membranes that separate them. Catch all the juice.

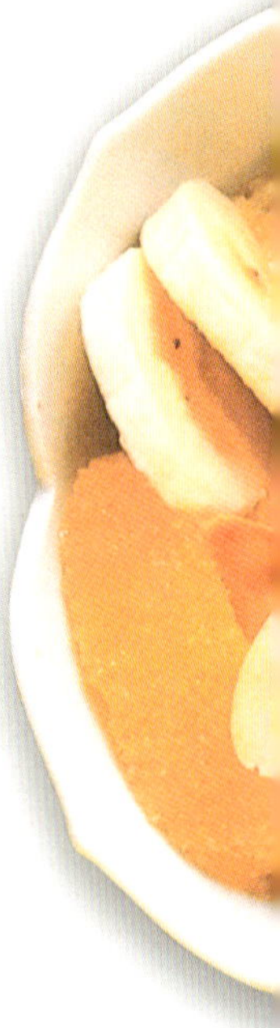

VARIATION: BANANA AND ORANGE COCKTAIL

2 oranges
2 bananas
2 tbsp slivered almonds, toasted

1 Remove the orange segments as for the grapefruit, then mix both citrus segments. (These may be covered and chilled ahead of time or overnight.) Just before serving, slice the bananas and mix them into the fruit. Spoon into dishes and top with almonds, then serve at once.

NUTRITIONAL VALUES

STRAWBERRIES WITH MELON AND ORANGE

SERVES **4**

This light and refreshing breakfast salad is the perfect start to hot summer days.

450 g halved strawberries

1 small melon, balled

2 oranges

125 ml orange juice (optional)

Mint leaves

NUTRITIONAL VALUES

1. Place the halved strawberries in a bowl with the melon balls. Peel the oranges, remove the pips and break into segments, then cut them in half or chop them roughly, depending on size.
2. Add the oranges to the other fruits with any juices, adding extra orange juice if necessary.
3. Leave to stand for 30 minutes. Serve the salad at room temperature, decorated with fresh mint leaves.

APRICOT GRANOLA

SERVES **8–10**

You can vary the granola mixture in many ways, substituting different nuts and seeds and using other dried fruits in place of the apricots. Do not store the granola until it has completely cooled or it will sweat and the ingredients will soften.

3 tbsp sunflower oil
6 tbsp clear honey
75 g rolled porridge oats
50 g rolled jumbo oats
50 g hazelnuts, chopped
25 g sunflower seeds
25 g sesame seeds
175 g dried apricots, chopped

1 Set the oven to 160°C/Gas mark 3. Melt the oil and the honey in a saucepan over a low heat. Stir in the oats, chopped nuts and seeds, mix well and immediately remove from the heat.

2 Spread the mixture on a baking tray and cook in the oven for 25 minutes, stirring from time to time with a wooden spoon. Remove the tray from the oven, stir in the chopped apricots and set aside to cool. When the mixture has thoroughly cooled, store in an airtight jar in a cool place.

3 You can serve the granola with a tempting variety of diary products and fruit juices. Try it with buttermilk, plain low-fat yoghurt or fromage frais mixed half-and-half with orange, apple or pineapple juice, or with fruit juice alone.

NUTRITIONAL VALUES

LIGHT MEALS

CUCUMBER SALAD WITH SPICED PORK AND SESAME SEEDS

SERVES **4**

1 small head Bok choy, shredded
1 medium cucumber, deseeded and diced
1 red pepper, deseeded and sliced
3 tbsp peanut oil
1 pork fillet (weighing about 0.5 kg), trimmed and sliced thin
1 tsp chilli sauce, or more according to taste
1 aubergine, sliced thin
1 red onion, sliced thin
1 garlic clove, sliced
1 green pepper, deseeded and sliced
2 tbsp light soy sauce
2 tbsp sesame seeds

1 Arrange the Bok choy and cucumber in a large salad bowl with the red pepper, then leave in a cool place until required.

2 Heat the oil in a large frying pan or wok, then add the pork fillet, and cook quickly to brown. Add the chilli sauce, then the aubergine, and stir-fry until the aubergine is beginning to brown. Add the remaining vegetables, and stir-fry briefly, then add the soy sauce. Scatter the sesame seeds into the pan, stir, then spoon the meat and vegetables over the prepared salad leaves. Toss lightly, then serve immediately.

NUTRITIONAL VALUES

SPINACH CRÊPES

SERVES **4**

These unusual light crêpes are made from a low-fat dough and rolled out. Keep an eye on them during cooking as they can quickly brown.

FOR THE CRÊPES

75 g flour

125 ml water

5 ml sunflower oil

FOR THE FILLING

2 tbsp vegetable stock

1 small courgette, sliced

50 g spinach, shredded

1 small onion chopped

65 g button mushrooms, sliced

½ red pepper, seeded and cut into strips

1 celery stick, sliced

1 garlic clove, crushed

a pinch of ground nutmeg

FOR THE SAUCE

150 ml skimmed milk

15 g cornflour

150 ml vegetable stock

ground black pepper

15 g low-fat vegetarian cheese, grated

½ tsp paprika

1 Sieve the flour for the crêpes into a mixing bowl and make a well in the centre. Heat the water and oil to boiling point and pour into the flour, mixing to form a dough. Turn on to a floured surface and knead for 3–4 minutes.

2 Cut the mixture into four equal portions and roll each into a 15 cm round. Heat a heavy, non-stick frying pan over medium heat. Put one of the crêpes into the plan and place another on top. Cook for 3–4 minutes, turning once the bottom crêpe begins to brown. Cover the cooked crêpes with a damp teatowel and repeat with the remaining mixture. Cover and reserve.

3 Heat the stock for the filling in a saucepan and cook the vegetables, garlic and nutmeg for 7–8 minutes, stirring. Drain the mixture well.

4 Blend 30 ml of the milk for the sauce to a paste with the cornflour. Put in a saucepan with the remaining milk, vegetable stock, seasoning, thyme and half of the cheese. Bring the mixture to the boil, stirring until thickened.

5 Heat the oven to 190°C/Gas mark 5. Spoon the vegetable mixture on to one half of each crêpe and roll up. Put in a shallow ovenproof dish, seam side down. Pour the sauce over the top and sprinkle with the remaining cheese and paprika. Cook in the oven for 15 minutes until golden brown. Serve immediately with salad.

NUTRITIONAL VALUES

ORANGE AND CHILLI MARINATED SARDINES

SERVES **4**

If liked, the sardines could be cooked on a barbecue for about 3–4 minutes once the coals are ready. It is best to place them in a hinged fish rack.

8–12 fresh sardines (depending on size), cleaned
120 ml orange juice
4 tbsp olive oil
4 green jalapeño chillies, deseeded and finely sliced
1 tsp soft brown sugar
few sprigs of fresh rosemary
orange wedges and sprigs of fresh rosemary, to garnish

1 Wipe or lightly rinse the sardines and pat dry with paper towels. Place in a shallow dish. Mix the orange juice, oil, chillies and sugar together and pour over the sardines. Tear the sprigs of rosemary into small pieces and scatter over the top. Cover and chill for at least 2 hours, turning the sardines occasionally.

2 Preheat the grill to medium and line the grill rack with foil. Drain the sardines and place on the foil-lined grill rack. Cook under the grill for 3–4 minutes, or until cooked, basting with the marinade at least once during cooking. Garnish with orange wedges and sprigs of rosemary.

NUTRITIONAL VALUES

CHICKPEAS IN YOGHURT SAUCE

SERVES **4**

This dish makes a lovely starter to a summer meal, and it is popular at parties, too. Poured over a jacket potato it makes a substantial meal.

240 ml low-fat natural yoghurt
75 g red and green peppers
75 g cucumber, chopped
2 spring onions, chopped
285 g chickpeas, tinned, drained
$^{1}/_{2}$ tsp chilli powder
1 clove garlic
$^{1}/_{2}$ tsp cumin seeds, crushed
1 tsp artificial sugar
salt and pepper to taste
1 tsp dried mint
2 tbsp coriander leaves or fresh mint or chives, chopped

1. Whisk 75–90 ml of water into the yoghurt to dilute it.
2. Wash, dry and chop the peppers.
3. Pour the chickpeas into the yoghurt. Add the chilli powder, garlic, cumin seeds, sugar and salt, and pepper and mix thoroughly. Add the vegetables and mint and mix again. Garnish with chopped coriander, mint or chives and chill well before serving.

NUTRITIONAL VALUES

MIXED VEGETABLE BHAJI

SERVES **4**

The best thing about this dish is that every time it is cooked, it has a new taste as the combination of the five vegetables is somehow never quite the same. It is also a very simple and quick way of making a bhaji and yet so tasty.

100 g green beans
175 g potatoes
100 g carrots
175 g aubergine
100 g tomatoes
1–2 green chillies
2 tbsp oil
7–8 cloves garlic, finely chopped
1/2 tsp chilli powder
1/4 tsp turmeric powder
1/2–3/4 tsp salt substitute (see page 12)
2–3 tbsp mint or coriander leaves

1. Top and tail and de-string the beans, then chop them into bite-size lengths.
2. Cut the potatoes into quarters and halve them again, preferably leaving the skin on.
3. Scrape and dice the carrots.
4. Cut the aubergine into four strips lengthwise and then slice across into 1 cm chunks.
5. Roughly chop the tomatoes and green chillies.
6. Measure the oil into a medium-sized heavy saucepan over a medium heat. Add the garlic, stirring it as soon as it begins to turn translucent, then add all the vegetables. Also stir in the chilli powder, turmeric and salt. Mix the spices together thoroughly.
7. Lower the heat, cover the pan and cook for another 20–25 minutes.
8. Add the mint or coriander leaves, stir and switch the heat off. Let it stand for 2–3 minutes before serving.

NUTRITIONAL VALUES

POTATO CHUNKS WITH FRESH SPINACH

SERVES **4**

This is an exceptionally good recipe for Bhajis, especially if a bunch of fresh fenugreek leaves is added to it.

- 400 g fresh or frozen leaf spinach
- 225 g potatoes
- 2 tbsp oil
- 1/4 tsp fenugreek seeds
- 1/2 tsp cumin seeds
- 60 g tomato, chopped
- 1/4 tsp turmeric
- 1/4 tsp chilli powder

1 If you are using fresh spinach, weigh it after you have removed the stalks and chopped it. Wash it thoroughly to remove all the hidden grit and leave to drain in a colander. If you are using frozen spinach, defrost it and let it drain well in a colander.

2 Scrub the potatoes well and do not peel them. Cut the potatoes into quarters, then cut each quarter into 2 or more pieces, making 8–12 pieces from each potato.

3 Heat the oil in a medium-sized heavy saucepan and fry the fenugreek and cumin seeds. As the seeds begin to sizzle, add the tomato, turmeric and chilli powder. Mix and cook the mixture for half a minute.

4 Add the spinach and potato and mix well so that the vegetables become well coated in the spices.

5 Cover the pan and simmer for 15–20 minutes. If there is still a little moisture left after this time, remove the lid and dry it out a little by cooking rapidly over a medium high heat for another few minutes, taking great care not to let it burn.

NUTRITIONAL VALUES

SARDINES COOKED WITH TOMATOES AND ROSEMARY

SERVES **8**

It has been said that once you have tasted this classic Greek dish, you'll dream of Greece forever.

8 fresh sardines, cleaned, head removed
flour for coating
olive oil for shallow frying

FOR THE SAUCE

4 tbsp olive oil
1 tbsp flour
60 ml red-wine vinegar
425 g tin chopped tomatoes
2 tsp rosemary, or 3 tsp chopped fresh rosemary
1 tsp dried oregano
2 garlic cloves, crushed
freshly ground black pepper, to taste
1 tsp sugar
fresh rosemary sprigs, to garnish
lemon wedges, to serve

1 Wash the sardines and pat dry with paper towels. Lay out on a chopping board and dredge with flour on both sides.

2 Heat the oil and cook the fish, in batches, for about 5 minutes, or until golden and cooked through. Using a slotted spoon, transfer the fish to a dish lined with paper towels to drain. Tent the fish with kitchen foil to keep warm.

3 To make the sauce, heat the olive oil in a medium-sized saucepan and stir in the flour to make a roux. Cook for 30 seconds, then gradually stir in the red-wine vinegar and add the chopped tomatoes, rosemary, oregano and garlic. Season with freshly ground black pepper and stir in the sugar. Cover and simmer for 15–20 minutes, until thickened, stirring occasionally.

4 Arrange the sardines on a warm serving platter and pour the sauce over them. Garnish with fresh rosemary sprigs and serve with lemon wedges.

NUTRITIONAL VALUES

SALMON WITH CORN RELISH

SERVES **4**

The colourful relish which accompanies this fish can be stored in the refrigerator; should you have any left over, serve chilled with other fish or meat such as plain pork or chicken.

900 g salmon fillet, cut into 4 equal pieces
2 sprigs fresh rosemary
1 garlic clove, peeled
freshly ground black pepper

FOR THE RELISH

2 corn on the cob
300 ml fish stock
1 small red pepper, seeded and finely chopped
1 small green chilli, chopped
2 spring onions, chopped
1 tbsp garlic wine vinegar
1 tbsp olive oil
2 tsp light brown sugar

NUTRITIONAL VALUES

1 Wash the fish under running water and pat dry. Arrange with the rosemary and garlic on a sheet of dampened greaseproof paper in the base of the steamer top. Season with pepper.

2 Put the corn cobs, stock, red pepper and chilli in the base of the steamer and bring to the boil.

3 Put the fish tier on top, cover with a tight-fitting lid and cook for 15–20 minutes. Remove the fish and keep warm, discarding the rosemary and garlic.

4 Remove the corn, red pepper and chilli from the stock. Cut the kernels from the corn cobs and transfer to a bowl with the chilli and red pepper, spring onions, vinegar, oil and sugar.

5 Boil the stock rapidly to reduce by half and add to the corn mixture.

6 Arrange the fish on a warmed serving plate. Garnish with the relish, and serve.

SALMON AND TOMATO PARCELS

SERVES **6**

Wrap salmon fillets in foil and cook them on the grill, and you'll be well on your way to a dinner with almost nothing to clean. Just crumple up the foil, throw it away and the dishes are done.

2 tsp unsalted butter
Six 4-cm thick skinless salmon fillets
6 tomatoes, cut into wedges
6 spring onions (white and green parts), chopped
2 tbsp olive oil
1 tbsp fresh lemon juice
1 tsp caster sugar
whole or chopped herbs, such as dill, coriander and parsley

NUTRITIONAL VALUES

1 Cut six large squares of heavy-duty foil. Butter the foil and lay a salmon fillet on each square. Top with some tomato wedges and a sprinkling of spring onions.

2 Whisk together the oil, lemon juice and sugar. Drizzle it over the salmon. Add a few sprigs of herbs to the parcels.

3 Close the parcels, being sure to secure the seams. Broil over medium–hot heat, turning occasionally, for 8–10 minutes. Carefully open the parcels to avoid the steam, and serve immediately.

VIETNAMESE CHICKEN NOODLE SOUP

SERVES **2**

A perfect brunch or late-night snack sold all over Vietnam by street vendors. Once a meal like this would have been based on beef, but modern-day versions use chicken or prawns.

3 celery sticks, finely chopped

3 spring onions with green tops, chopped into rings

300 g cooked chicken, skinned and cut into fine strips

2 pieces of light wood ear fungus, or 8 white button mushrooms

225 g steamed flat rice noodles, or dried rice stick noodles

850 ml chicken stock

1. Place the celery and spring onions in a bowl, and the chicken in another bowl. Place both on the table. If using wood ear fungus, soak it in hot water for 20–30 minutes.
2. Cook the noodles following the instructions on the packet. Rinse and drain then divide the noodles among four bowls.
3. In a pan, bring the stock to a simmer and add the wood ear fungi. Cook for 3–5 minutes. Pour into a bowl and place on the table.
4. To eat, place celery, spring onions and chicken onto the noodles, and ladle on the chicken and mushroom stock.

NUTRITIONAL VALUES

BAKED TUNA PASTA

SERVES **4**

This classic dish is delicious and easy to prepare.

300 g dried pasta shapes

FOR THE BECHAMEL SAUCE

600 ml soya milk

1 sprig parsley

10 black peppercorns

2 slices of onion

2 bay leaves

2 blades of mace

60 g soya margarine

40 g plain flour

1 medium onion, chopped

1 tbsp tomato purée

1 tbsp tomato ketchup

1 tbsp chopped fresh parsley

black pepper

1 x 400 g tins tuna

1 red pepper, chopped

100 g frozen peas

1 Boil the pasta in a pan of boiling water until *al dente* (firm to the bite). Drain well.

2 Make the bechamel sauce adding the onion slices after you melt the margarine in the pan, then fry for 3–4 minutes. Add the flour and blend in well. Add the milk a little at a time, mixing well with a spoon each time you add it. Repeat until all the milk has been used.

3 Add the tomato purée and ketchup and the chopped parsley; season with black pepper to taste. Heat the oven to 190°C/gas mark 5.

4 Add the tuna, pepper, peas and pasta and mix well.

5 Pour the mixture into an ovenproof dish and bake for 30–35 minutes until lightly browned. Serve hot.

NUTRITIONAL VALUES

TUNA WHOLEWHEAT ROLLS

SERVES **4**

An anytime, anywhere dish that is easily prepared in minutes.

4 wholewheat rolls, crusty
25 g polyunsaturated margarine
2 spring onions, washed and sliced
4 mushrooms, washed and sliced
1 small tin tuna fish, drained
4 tbsp tinned or cooked corn kernels
2 tsp lemon juice
$^1/_2$ tsp paprika
freshly ground pepper

1 Cut a round from the top of each roll about 4 cm in diameter and scoop out some of the inside.

2 Melt the polyunsaturated margarine in a small frying pan, add the sliced onions, and sliced mushrooms. Allow to cook over a low heat for 2 minutes.

3 Remove from the heat and stir in the remaining ingredients, including the breadcrumbs from the roll. Season to taste.

4 Stuff the rolls with the filling and replace the lids. Wrap in a square of foil and allow to heat for 10 minutes. Remove from the oven and unwrap the foil.

5 Serve with a crispy green salad for a snack lunch.

NUTRITIONAL VALUES

TROUT STUFFED WITH TABBOULEH

SERVES **4**

Whole trout bakes very successfully in a claypot. This dish of tender fish, bulgur wheat, diced salad vegetables and the fresh flavours of mint and parsley, is perfect for a light summer lunch or supper.

four 250 g trout, cleaned and heads removed
black pepper
4 tbsp dry white wine
lemon wedges, mint and parsley, to garnish

FOR THE STUFFING

100 g bulgur wheat, soaked according to the manufacturer's instructions
50 g finely diced cucumber
4 medium tomatoes, seeded and finely chopped
2 tbsp chopped mint
2 tbsp chopped parsley
1 tbsp lemon juice
60 ml plain low-fat yoghurt

1. Presoak a claypot and line the bottom with waxed paper. Wash the trout inside and out, and pat dry using paper towels. Season the cavities with pepper and set aside.

2. For the stuffing, mix all the ingredients together, except the yoghurt, and reserving some mint and parsley for garnish, to serve and season. Spoon some stuffing into the cavity of each trout and transfer them to the claypot. Any remaining stuffing mixture can be chilled and served as a salad accompaniment. Spoon the white wine over the trout, cover, and place in a cold oven. Set the oven to 220°C/gas mark 7, and cook for 45 minutes or until the trout are done.

3. Just before the end of cooking, blend the yoghurt, mint, parsley and seasoning together. Carefully remove the trout from the pot, garnish with lemon wedges, mint leaves and sprigs of parsley, and serve with the sauce.

NUTRITIONAL VALUES

FLAGEOLET BEANS WITH SPINACH

SERVES **4**

This no-fuss dish is ideal for summer days when spare time is best spent outdoors rather than slaving for hours in a hot kitchen.

450 g fresh spinach, trimmed and washed

2 tbsp olive oil

6 spring onions, chopped

2 x 425 g tins flageolet beans, drained

2 small courgettes, trimmed and thinly sliced

2 tbsp chopped fresh mint

several large basil sprigs, leaves shredded

225 g feta cheese, crumbled

salt substitute (see page 12)

freshly ground black pepper

1 Press all the spinach leaves into a large saucepan while still dripping wet. Put a lid on the pan and place it over high heat. Cook, shaking the pan often, for about 5 minutes, or until the spinach has wilted and shrunk. Stir the leaves, cover, and cook for a further 2 minutes or so, until tender. Drain well, then replace the spinach in the pan. Cover and leave over low heat to keep hot.

2 Heat the oil, then stir-fry the spring onions, flageolet beans and courgettes for 5 minutes, until the courgettes are just cooked. Spoon the spinach on to one large or four individual serving plates. Toss the mint, basil and feta into the vegetables, and add seasoning to taste. Spoon the vegetables over the spinach and serve the dish at once.

NUTRITIONAL VALUES

FRIED MARINATED HERRINGS

SERVES **2**

This is an easy-to-prepare and quick meal. Marinating the herrings in sake *and soy sauce adds extra flavour.*

2 large or small 4 herrings, gutted and boned

2 tbsp plain flour

2 tbsp vegetable oil

FOR THE MARINADE

4 tsp *sake*

4 tsp soy sauce

FOR THE DRESSING

4 tsp soy sauce

2 tsp wine vinegar

1 tsp caster sugar

1. Mix together the *sake* and soy sauce, then pour over the herrings and marinate for 30 minutes, turning 2 or 3 times.
2. Meanwhile, make the dressing by mixing the soy sauce, vinegar and sugar in a bowl.
3. Wipe the herrings with absorbent kitchen paper and then coat with the flour.
4. Heat the vegetable oil in a frying pan and fry the herrings for about 3 minutes on each side or until the flour coating is golden brown. Serve with rice and a vegetable dish.

NUTRITIONAL VALUES

APPLE AND WALNUT SALAD

SERVES **2**

This refreshing, crisp summer salad provides the perfect accompaniment to a glass (or two) of chilled Spanish sherry. For a tangier version, add a dash of lemon juice to the mayonnaise before mixing it into the salad.

- 1 large sweet green apple
- 3 tbsp lemon juice
- 3 spring onions, chopped
- 35 g sultanas
- 1 celery stalk, trimmed and chopped
- 2 medium cooked potatoes, peeled and chopped
- 8 walnuts, shelled
- 225 ml low-fat mayonnaise
- 1 1/4 tbsp chopped coriander

1 Peel, core and dice the apple. Sprinkle with a little lemon juice to prevent discoloration and set aside. Combine the spring onions, sultanas, celery and potatoes in a medium earthenware bowl. Add the diced apple, walnuts and low-fat mayonnaise, mixing thoroughly. Sprinkle lightly with coriander and serve immediately.

NUTRITIONAL VALUES

CATALAN ROASTED VEGETABLE SALAD

SERVES **4**

The Catalan name for this recipe, escalivada, *comes from the verb* escalivar, *meaning 'to cook over hot embers'. It is a colourful array of vegetables, roasted to perfection and glistening with olive oil, which is usually served on a rustic, earthenware platter.*

2 medium yellow onions, unpeeled
1 medium (450 g) aubergine
1 large green pepper
1 large red pepper
2 medium tomatoes
8 cloves garlic
2 tsp cumin seeds
2 tbsp lemon juice
3 tbsp sherry vinegar
4 tbsp olive oil
1 tsp sweet paprika
1 tsp chopped fresh rosemary

NUTRITIONAL VALUES

1 Lay the onions on a baking sheet and bake in the oven at 180°C/gas mark 4 for 10 minutes. Add the aubergine and bake for a further 10 minutes. Add the peppers, tomatoes and half of the garlic cloves and bake until all vegetables are tender. Remove the vegetables from the oven and allow to cool.

2 Peel the vegetables with your fingers. Cut the aubergine into strips. Remove the stem, core and remove seeds from the peppers, and cut into strips as well. Seed the tomatoes, then slice into wedges. Thinly slice the onion. Arrange the vegetables attractively on a serving platter.

3 In a food processor, combine the roasted garlic, the remaining cloves of raw garlic, the cumin seeds, lemon juice, vinegar, olive oil, paprika and rosemary. When the mixture is smooth, pour it evenly over the vegetables and serve.

TAPA OF ROASTED PEPPERS WITH TUNA

SERVES **3–4**

Based on escalivada *(see page 52), this light, refreshing tapa combines ease and elegance in equal parts. The vinaigrette seems almost too easy to prepare, yet it zestily dresses the roasted vegetables to perfection. Oil-infused tuna and hard-boiled eggs add protein to this crisp Mediterranean dish.*

3 medium green peppers
3 medium red peppers
2 large tomatoes, skinned, seeded and diced
½ small yellow onion, diced
8 tbsp olive oil
6 tbsp red wine vinegar
½ tsp pepper
2 hard-boiled eggs, shelled and sliced
175 g tinned tuna, packed in olive oil

1. Char the peppers under a grill until they are blackened on all sides. Wrap in a paper bag and allow to stand for 10–15 minutes to steam. Peel, seed and cut into long, thin strips, then transfer to a bowl. Add the tomatoes and onion, and set aside.

2. In a medium bowl, whisk together the olive oil, vinegar and pepper. Pour this mixture over the vegetables and combine well, coating all vegetables with the dressing.

3. Transfer the vegetables to a serving dish and top with the sliced hard-boiled eggs and tuna.

NUTRITIONAL VALUES

WILTED MIZUNA WITH WALNUTS

SERVES **4**

Mizuna is a wonderful raw ingredient in salads, but wilting it slightly with a dressing makes for a delectable variation. In this recipe, some red cabbage and green beans have been added for colour, but you can use your imagination to zest it up.

1 tbsp olive oil
1 red onion, sliced
3 cloves garlic, peeled and crushed
120 g green beans, julienned
120 g red cabbage, julienned
120 g mizuna or spinach, chopped coarsely
3 tbsp rice vinegar
50 g walnuts, chopped

NUTRITIONAL VALUES

1. Heat the olive oil in a pan on a medium heat and sauté the onion and garlic for 1 minute.
2. Add the green beans and sauté for 1 minute or until the colour becomes darker.
3. Add the red cabbage and sauté for a further minute.
4. Add the mizuna or spinach and sauté for another minute. Stir in the vinegar and remove from the heat.
5. Combine the vegetables with the walnuts and serve immediately.

STARTERS

AVOCADO AND POMEGRANATE SALAD

SERVES **4**

Avocados are Israel's top export, and are so popular and plentiful that they are used in many salads and appetizer dishes. Oranges, also a big export fruit, and pomegranates combine perfectly in this salad, which makes an unusual first course or a side dish for a meat or dairy dinner.

4 tbsp white-wine vinegar
3 tbsp orange juice
salt substitute (see page 12)
freshly ground black pepper
1 tsp honey
2 tbsp olive oil
1 tbsp peanut or sunflower oil
2 tbsp chopped fresh mint
1 ripe pomegranate, cut in half and pips removed
2 ripe avocados
1 tbsp lemon juice
fresh mint leaves to garnish

1 In a small bowl, whisk together wine vinegar, orange juice, salt substitute, pepper to taste and honey. Slowly whisk in olive oil and vegetable oil until dressing is thick and creamy. Stir in the chopped mint. Set aside.

2 Into a medium bowl, scrape seeds out of pomegranate halves. Add grapes and toss to mix.

3 Cut avocados in half and remove stones. Using a round-bladed knife, run it between skin and flesh of avocados, working skin away from flesh until skin is removed.

4 Place avocados, round-side up, on work surface and, using a sharp knife and starting 1.25 cm below stalk end, cut avocado lengthwise into 6 mm slices, leaving stalk end intact. Arrange each sliced avocado in half on four individual plates. Using palm of hand, gently push avocado slices forwards to fan out slices. Sprinkle lemon juice over them.

5 Sprinkle one-quarter of the pomegranate seed-grape mixture on to each avocado half and spoon over dressing. Garnish each plate with a few mint leaves.

NUTRITIONAL VALUES

AVOCADO, GRAPEFRUIT AND PRAWN SALAD

SERVES **4**

The pink of prawns and grapefruit, with the green of avocado, makes a cheerful, refreshing salad to enjoy when the weather is hot.

2 grapefruit

2 avocados

225 g prawns or shrimps

150 ml French dressing

NUTRITIONAL VALUES

1 To make the grapefruit sections, place the fruit in a bowl and pour boiling water on top to cover. Leave for 2 minutes, then remove and allow to cool. Cut a slice from the top of the fruit, then cut the peel and pith off in strips to reveal the flesh. It is essential to use a small, sharp knife.

2 When all the pith has been cut away, remove each section by cutting between the membranes of each segment. At the end only the tough outer skin should be left and each section of fruit should be separate without skin.

3 Peel the avocados, cut in half lengthways and remove the stones. Cut the flesh into slices.

4 Arrange the avocado slices, grapefruit segments and prawns or shrimps in dishes and serve with French dressing. The dressing may be poured over the salad or served separately.

AVOCADO FISH

SERVES **4**

Tuna is high in protein and low in fat and calories when compared with other proteins, and when teamed up with avocado makes a very satisfying starter.

2 avocados
juice of 1 lemon
100 g tuna fish
150 ml natural yoghurt
1 tsp cumin powder
1 clove garlic, crushed
50 g long-grain rice

GARNISH

rind of lemon
1/4 tsp paprika
prawns

1 Slice the avocados lengthways. Remove the stones. Remove some of the flesh and sprinkle lemon juice into the shells and onto the flesh.

2 Mix the tuna fish with the diced avocado flesh.

3 In a small bowl mix the yoghurt, cumin and crushed garlic. Stir well. Add the cooked rice and the avocado and fish mixture.

4 Arrange the filling in the avocado shells.

5 Garnish with lemon rind, paprika and prawns.

NUTRITIONAL VALUES

TUNA AND AUBERGINE KEBABS

SERVES **4**

Broaden your use of this interesting vegetable by combining it with tuna to make these unusual kebabs.

567 g fresh tuna steak, cut into 2.5 cm cubes

1 long, thin, Japanese-style aubergine

MARINADE

grated rind and juice of 1 lime

1 tbsp olive oil

1 garlic clove, chopped finely

2 tbsp fresh oregano and parsley, finely chopped

salt substitute (see page 12)

freshly ground black pepper

1 Place tuna in a non-metallic bowl, then add all marinade ingredients. Stir well and leave for at least 1 hour, stirring once or twice.

2 Half cook the aubergine on a barbecue or under a grill, until skin is just starting to wrinkle. Cut into 1.25 cm thick slices.

3 Soak kebab sticks in water to prevent them charring under the grill. Thread tuna and aubergine on skewers, then brush with remaining marinade.

4 Cook under a moderate heat for 5 or 6 minutes on each side, either on a barbecue or under the grill, basting at intervals with any remaining marinade. Serve alone or with a rice salad.

NUTRITIONAL VALUES

SMOKED MACKEREL PÂTÉ

SERVES **4**

The fromage frais and low-fat cottage cheese replace the cream, butter or full-fat soft cheese often used for making pâtés.

225 g smoked mackerel, skinned, boned and flaked

100 g fromage frais

100 g low-fat cottage cheese

1 tsp grated horseradish

1 tbsp lemon juice

pepper

1 tbsp fresh parsley, chopped

1 tbsp dry wholemeal breadcrumbs

GARNISH

lime wedges

radicchio leaves

1. Place the fish, fromage frais, low-fat cottage cheese, horseradish and lemon juice in a food processor or blender and mix until smooth.

2. Season with pepper, add the parsley and breadcrumbs and blend together. Spoon into a dish and chill for 30 minutes.

3. Serve individual portions, garnished with lime and radicchio. Serve toasted wholewheat bread triangles separately.

NUTRITIONAL VALUES

SARDINE-STUFFED LEMONS

SERVES **6**

Sardines, like lentils, are a traditional food of the poor, which now have considerable cachet among the foodies. This is a different presentation, eaten as a light lunch or a European-style first course.

3 plump round lemons
2 x 150 g tins sardines packed in olive oil, drained
3 tbsp low-fat mayonnaise
1½ tbsp Dijon mustard
1 large celery stalk, finely chopped
4 spring onions, finely chopped
2 tbsp finely chopped flat-leaved parsley
freshly ground pepper
2 tbsp pine nuts
green olives, cut lengthways into slivers

NUTRITIONAL VALUES

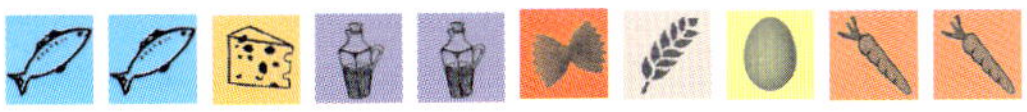

1 Halve the lemons and squeeze them with a juicer, reserve the juice. Take each half and carefully cut a thin slice from the bottom so that it will stand. With your fingers, try to remove as much as possible of the inner membrane from each half. Place the halves upside down for a few minutes.

2 Meanwhile, decant the drained sardines into a bowl. Mash together with the low-fat mayonnaise, mustard, and 2 tablespoons of the lemon juice. Try to obtain a fairly smooth paste. Work in the chopped celery, onions and parsley. Season to taste and give a final stir.

3 Divide the sardine paste among the six lemon halves, shape the tops attractively and garnish with a few toasted pine nuts and slivers of green olive. Chill briefly (for up to 2 hours) and serve with warm *khoubz* (Arab bread) or pitta.

SEAWEED-WRAPPED AVOCADO

SERVES **2**

Avocado is not a traditional ingredient of Japanese cooking but it is certainly popular in many Japanese homes. This popularity is said to be due to the similarity between the taste of the avocado and the taste of raw tuna as used in sushi *and* sashimi. *You can mix in* wasabi, *the green Japanese mustard powder, to spice up the soy sauce, which can be used as a dressing, if you wish.*

- 1 avocado
- 2 sheets of dried seaweed (*nori*)
- 2 tsp soy sauce
- 1 tsp *wasabi* (optional)

NUTRITIONAL VALUES

1. Slice the avocado in two, remove the stone and peel. Cut in half again, then slice into 1.25 cm widths.
2. Cut the *nori* into strips and wrap the avocado slices in the *nori*.
3. Pour soy sauce into a small dish. If you are using *wasabi*, mash in a small amount. Dip the avocado into the sauce before eating.

ARTICHOKES BRAISED WITH HERBS AND OLIVE OIL

SERVES **4–6**

Artichokes, stuffed with mint, parsley and garlic, then braised with olive oil and lemon, are one of the delights of the Roman kitchen. They make a marvellous antipasto, and left-overs are delicious, too, when added to braised meats, or sliced and served with roasted fish or chicken.

An artichoke is a big thistle plant that is native to the Mediterranean.

25 g finely chopped parsley
2–3 tbsp finely chopped, fresh mint leaves, or more as desired
8–10 garlic cloves, finely chopped
salt substitute (see page 12)
freshly ground black pepper
120 ml extra-virgin olive oil
8 medium-sized artichokes
juice of 1 lemon

1 Preheat the oven to 180°C/gas mark 4. Combine the parsley with the mint, garlic, salt substitute and pepper, and about 3 tablespoons of the olive oil or enough to form a paste. Leave aside to marinate while you prepare the artichokes.

2 Remove the hard leaves from the artichokes, and cut away the sharp top from the tender, inner leaves. Pull the centre open, and scoop out the thistly part inside, using a spoon and a sharp paring knife.

3 Stuff the inside of each artichoke with the herby mixture, then lay the artichokes in a baking dish in a single layer. Sprinkle with salt substitute, pepper, and any left-over herby mixture, then sprinkle with the remaining olive oil and lemon juice, adding enough water to cover the artichokes. Cover with a lid or with foil.

4 Bake for about 1 hour. Remove the lid to taste the sauce. If it lacks flavour, pour it into a saucepan and reduce until it condenses and intensifies – you want the liquid to be evaporated to isolate the flavourful oil. Once that has happened, stop boiling immediately. Season with salt substiute, pepper and lemon juice, then pour it back over the artichokes. Serve hot or cold.

NUTRITIONAL VALUES

MEDITERRANEAN SALSA

SERVES **4**

Serve this salsa warm as part of a meal, or toss it into a pan of freshly cooked pasta.

1 large aubergine

4 long spring onions, quartered

2 plum tomatoes, quartered

1 tbsp olive oil

freshly ground black pepper

DRESSING

3 tbsp olive oil

juice of ½ lemon

1 tbsp chopped fresh oregano

NUTRITIONAL VALUES

1. Preheat the grill to high. Slice the aubergine into 1.25 cm rounds and place on a foil-lined grill pan with the spring onions and tomatoes. Brush with olive oil and sprinkle with freshly ground black pepper.

2. Place the vegetables under the grill for 8–10 minutes, turning once, until tender and lightly charred. Cut the aubergine slices into cubes and place in a large bowl with the spring onions and tomatoes.

3. Quickly whisk together the dressing ingredients and pour over the warm vegetables. Toss well together and season with black pepper to taste.

MEDITERRANEAN FISH SOUP

SERVES **4**

This fish soup gives you the opportunity to savour all the flavours of the Mediterranean.

- 4 tbsp olive oil
- 1 large onion, finely chopped
- 2 cloves garlic, crushed
- 2 celery sticks, sliced
- 395 g tins of tomatoes, chopped
- 200 ml dry white wine
- 590 ml boiling water
- salt substitute (see page 12)
- freshly ground black pepper
- 500 g mussels, scrubbed and beards removed
- 0.5 kg white fish fillets, skinned and cut into chunks
- 1 mackerel, skinned, filleted and cut into chunks
- 113 g shelled cooked prawns
- chopped fresh parsley, to garnish

1. Place the oil, onion and garlic in a microwave-safe bowl and cook on full for 4 minutes.
2. Add the celery and tomatoes, wine, water and salt substitute and pepper. Cook on full for 15 minutes.
3. Discard any opened mussels. Ladle a little of the soup broth into a separate large, microwave-safe bowl and place the washed mussels in it. Cover and cook on full for 5–8 minutes, stirring once. Discard any unopened mussels, then add the rest to the soup.
4. Place the white fish and mackerel in another microwave-safe dish, cover, and cook on FULL for 3–4 minutes, or until firm. Add to the soup with the shrimp. Cook on FULL for 1–2 minutes to heat before serving, garnished with chopped parsley.

NUTRITIONAL VALUES

SICILIAN TOMATOES

SERVES **4–8**

Firm round, beef tomatoes are perfect for stuffing with the flavours of the Mediterranean, either as a starter or as a supper dish. Try tuna fish as an alternative to chicken.

8 beef tomatoes
2 tbsp olive oil
1 medium onion, finely chopped
1 clove garlic, crushed (minced)
15 g pinenuts
50 g fresh white breadcrumbs
175 g cooked chicken, finely chopped or minced
2 tbsp fresh oregano or marjoram
2 tsp capers, chopped
4 black olives, chopped
salt substitute (see page 12)
freshly ground black pepper
dash Tabasco
25 g Parmesan cheese, freshly grated

1 Slice the top of each tomato and scoop out the pulp and seeds; chop and reserve these for later.

2 Heat the oil in a pan and gently cook the onion, garlic and pinenuts, until the onion is softened and the nuts golden brown.

3 Stir in the breadcrumbs and chicken. Cook for a further minute. Remove from the heat and stir in the oregano or marjoram, capers, olives, salt substitute and pepper to taste. Stir in the tomato pulp and add a dash of Tabasco sauce.

4 Spoon the stuffing mixture back into the tomato shells. Sprinkle with the Parmesan cheese.

5 Place the tomatoes on a greased baking tray and cook for 20–30 minutes at 180°C/gas mark 4 or until tender and the Parmesan is golden. Serve warm.

NUTRITIONAL VALUES

CURLY ENDIVE AND ALFALFA SALAD

SERVES **4**

It is easy to grow the crisp and crunchy alfalfa seed sprouts yourself, but you can also buy them in health food shops and specialist greengrocery stores. Use them in salads of all kinds as an accompaniment, or even as a snack. Like other sprouted seeds, they are an excellent source of the B and C vitamins, and also high in fibre.

1/2 small curly endive, torn into pieces
100 g alfalfa sprouts
50 g small button mushrooms, trimmed and thinly sliced
1/2 red pepper, cored, seeded and sliced

DRESSING

juice of 1 lemon
2 tsp sunflower oil
1 small onion, grated
1/4 tsp Chinese five-spice powder

1 Arrange the endive leaves on a large serving plate or four individual plates. Mix the alfalfa, mushrooms and pepper together in a bowl.

2 Mix the dressing ingredients together and add to the bowl of vegetables. Toss well and, just before serving, arrange on top of the endive leaves.

NUTRITIONAL VALUES

PEPPER AND AUBERGINE PÂTÉ

SERVES **4**

Known in its native Bulgaria as Ajvar, *this reddish-coloured pâté derives its creamy consistency and smoked flavour from the fire-roasted aubergine. Serve with a selection of crudités such as cucumbers, spring onions or sweet peppers.*

- 1 each: red, orange, yellow pepper, diced
- 3 tbspl extra-virgin olive oil
- 4 to 5 cloves garlic, sliced thin
- 1 aubergine
- black and cayenne pepper to taste
- $\frac{1}{2}$ tsp lemon juice, or to taste
- few sprigs of parsley to garnish

1 Sweat the peppers in the olive oil, then add the garlic. When the peppers are very soft remove from the heat.

2 Meanwhile, roast the aubergine, either in the oven (preheat the oven to 200°C/gas mark 6), or, for a richer flavour, over a gas flame or on a barbecue. Turn the aubergine occasionally to char the vegetable evenly and when it appears to have deflated from the inside transfer it to a bowl and cover it. Allow to cool, about 30 minutes.

3 Remove the skin from the aubergine, reserving the juices, and dice the flesh.

4 Return the peppers to the heat and add the aubergine flesh and the juices. Cook over medium-low heat for 5 to 8 minutes or until the mixture loses some of its moisture and thickens slightly.

5 Purée the vegetable mixture in a blender or food processor, then season with black and cayenne pepper, and lemon juice to taste. Serve garnished with sprigs of parsley.

NUTRITIONAL VALUES

RED PEPPER SOUP

SERVES **4**

This vibrantly coloured soup, from the South of France, is scented with the Provençal flavours of garlic, tomatoes, fennel and herbs. If the weather is hot, serve it chilled rather than hot.

- 5 shallots, chopped
- 3 cloves garlic, chopped
- 2 tbsp olive oil
- 2 red peppers, chopped
- 250 g tomatoes, chopped (or 400 ml can tomatoes, including the juices)
- 1 tbsp Pernod or ouzo, if preferred a pinch of anise or fennel seeds can be added
- 2 tsp paprika
- 1/2 tsp herbes de Provence
- 500 ml chicken or vegetable broth
- 250 ml low-fat crème fraîche
- fresh thyme sprig to garnish

NUTRITIONAL VALUES

1 Lightly sauté the shallots and garlic in the olive oil until soft, then add the peppers and cook over medium–low heat until the peppers are soft.

2 Add the tomatoes, Pernod, paprika, herbes de Provence and broth to cook over medium–high heat until mixture comes to the boil.

3 Purée the soup, leaving a little texture of the red peppers to the mixture. Stir half the low-fat crème fraîche into a bowl, then add several spoonfuls of the soup to it, mixing until smooth. Add this mixture to the soup, keeping it on the heat just long enough to warm it through.

4 Serve garnished with a spoonful of the remaining crème fraîche and a sprig of thyme.

MACKEREL IN WHITE WINE

SERVES **4**

Use a dry white wine, preferably a Muscadet, for this recipe. The mackerel can be served as a simple but delicious appetizer, accompanied by slices of fresh, low-salt white bread.

- 2 medium onions
- 2 small carrots
- 2 unwaxed lemons, sliced
- 1 tbsp olive oil
- 2 sprigs rosemary
- 2 sprigs thyme
- 1 bay leaf
- 2 cloves
- 2 mackerel, cleaned and gutted
- 150 ml dry white whine (e.g. Muscadet)
- salt substitute (see page 12)
- freshly ground black pepper

NUTRITIONAL VALUES

1. Peel and slice the onions and carrots. Cut the lemons into slices. Heat the oil in a skillet, then lightly brown the carrots, onions, the slices from one of the lemons, one rosemary and one thyme sprig, the bay leaf and cloves for 5 minutes.
2. Add the mackerel and cover with the wine. Season and cook for 15 minutes over a gentle heat.
3. Remove from the heat and arrange the mackerel on a serving dish using the remaining lemon slices as a garnish.
4. Strain the cooking liquor and pour over the mackerel.
5. Allow to cool completely before serving. Garnish with the remaining rosemary and thyme sprigs.

HERRING WITH MIXED ONION SALAD

SERVES **4**

Onions mixed with herrings and sour cream is a typical Scandinavian cold-table dish which makes a great starter. You can add any roe to this recipe – fry with the herrings for 2–3 minutes.

4 large herrings or 2 mackerel, filleted
salt substitute (see page 12)
freshly ground black pepper
4 tbsp oat flour or wholewheat flour
3 tbsp peanut oil
2 heads Boston lettuce, washed and broken into bite-size pieces
2 handfuls watercress
1 large apple, cored and sliced
1 tbsp lemon juice
1 red onion, cut into rings
4 tbsp sour cream
1 to 2 spring onions, trimmed and chopped finely

NUTRITIONAL VALUES

1. Season the herring fillets well, then turn them in the flour to coat.
2. Heat the oil in a large frying pan, add the fillets skin side up and cook for 3-4 minutes, depending on size.
3. Meanwhile, arrange the lettuce and watercress on plates. Toss the apple in lemon juice and arrange on the leaves.
4. Turn the herrings and cook for a further 2-3 minutes (add any roe at this stage, if using).
5. Arrange the onions rings on the salad.
6. Cut the herrings into bite-size pieces and arrange on the salad. Add the sour cream, top with the chopped spring onions and serve.

PRAWN AND HOT PEPPER TAPAS

SERVES **4**

Prawn tapas are a treat, sizzling in their ceramic bowl, redolent of garlic and hot peppers, and perfect for nibbling out of their shells as you chat and drink and enjoy the evening.

500–700 g large prawns, in their shells
5–8 cloves garlic, chopped
large pinch hot pepper flakes
1 lemon
5–6 tbsp olive oil
200 ml dry white wine
1–2 tbsp fresh chopped flat leaf parsley

1. Combine the prawns with half the garlic, hot pepper flakes, juice of half the lemon and half the olive oil. Sprinkle with salt to taste; leave to marinate for at least 30 minutes. Meanwhile, cut the remaining half lemon into wedges and set aside.

2. Heat a frying pan until very hot. Add the remaining olive oil and garlic, cook for a moment or two, then reduce the heat and add the prawns to the skillet. Cook for a few minutes, turning occasionally, until the prawns are opaque.

3. Remove the prawns from the frying pan, place on a plate and cover to keep warm. Pour in the wine and boil down until reduced to only a few spoonfuls of intensely flavoured sauce, then pour it over the prawns.

4. Serve hot, sprinkled with parsley and lemon wedges for squeezing over the prawns.

NUTRITIONAL VALUES

MAIN COURSES

TURKEY, TOMATO AND BASIL LASAGNE

SERVES **4**

Use finely chopped turkey breast, or if preferred, chopped or minced chicken breast to make this tasty lasagne.

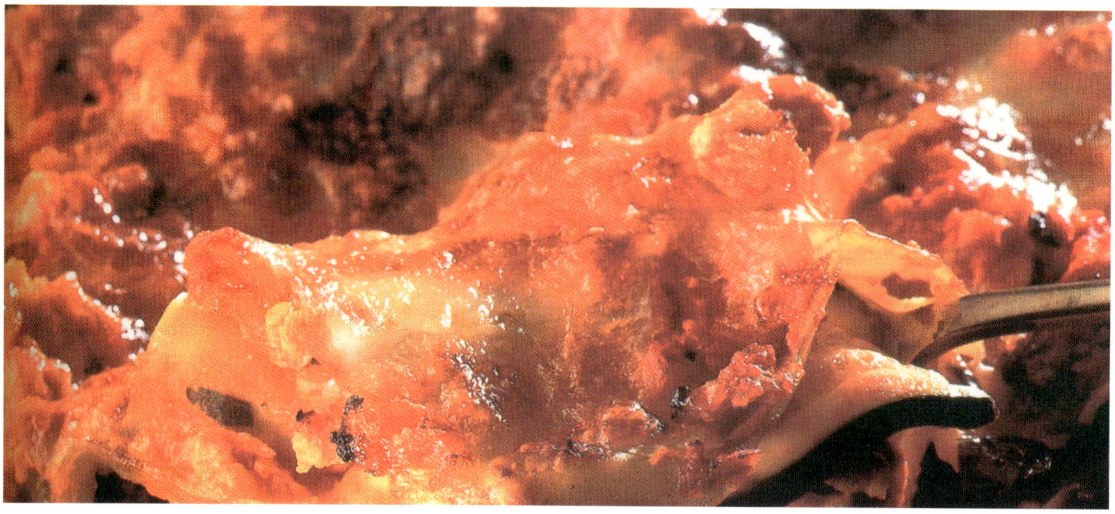

- 2 tbsp olive oil
- 1 large onion, peeled and finely chopped
- 2–3 garlic cloves, crushed
- 350 g minced turkey
- 400 g tin chopped tomatoes
- salt substitute (see page 12) and black pepper
- 2 tbsp chopped fresh basil
- 6–8 fresh lasagne verdi sheets
- 225 g courgettes
- 50 g grated mozzarella cheese
- fresh basil sprigs, to garnish

1 Preheat the oven to 190°C/gas mark 5, 10 minutes before baking the lasagne. Heat the oil in a large pan and sauté the onion and garlic for 5 minutes or until the onion is softened Add the minced turkey and continue to sauté for a further 5 minutes or until sealed.

2 Add the tomatoes, bring to the boil, then reduce the heat and simmer for 10 minutes or until a thick consistency is formed. Season to taste and stir in the basil.

NUTRITIONAL VALUES

3 Bring a large pan of water to the boil, add 1 tablespoon salt substitute, then drop in four lasagne sheets, one at a time. Cook for 2–3 minutes, ensuring that they do not stick together. Drain, lay them on clean teatowels and pat dry. Repeat with the remaining lasagne sheets.

4 Place about a third of the sauce in the base of an ovenproof dish and cover with a layer of blanched courgette slices, then 3–4 lasagne sheets. Repeat the layering, finishing with a layer of sauce. Sprinkle with the grated cheese. Bake the lasagne in the oven for 20–25 minutes or until the cheese is golden. Serve garnished with fresh basil sprigs.

TUNA WITH MANGO SALSA

SERVES **4**

This recipe, using a mango salsa, would work well with swordfish or salmon. Beat the refried beans so that they are not too lumpy.

1 tbsp sunflower oil
3 tbsp white wine
426 g tin refried beans
4 tuna steaks, each about 150 g
salt substitute (see page 12) and freshly ground black pepper
1 small ripe mango, peeled and finely chopped
1–2 green jalapeño chillies, deseeded and chopped
2 tbsp chopped fresh coriander
flat leaf parsley sprigs, to garnish
cooked rice and salad, to serve

1 Preheat a slow cooker on high. Lightly oil the cooking pot with the sunflower oil. Place the wine and beans into the cooking pot and heat through while preparing the remaining ingredients. Lightly rinse the tuna steaks, pat dry, season and reserve. Stir together the mango, shallots, chillies, garlic, tomatoes and coriander.

2 Beat the refried beans in the cooking pot until smooth, then place the tuna on top of the beans. Spoon over the mango salsa. Cover and cook on low for 3–4 hours. Garnish with parsley sprigs and serve with freshly cooked rice and a salad.

NUTRITIONAL VALUES

CARIBBEAN SEARED TUNA

SERVES **4**

This recipe is a wonderful example of how a small amount of oil can give a lovely, large amount of flavour. Serve with sweet potatoes.

4 tuna teams, about 175 g each
3 garlic cloves
1/2 tsp cumin
juice of 2 limes, or juice of 1 orange and 1 lime
black and cayenne pepper to taste
2 tbsp extra virgin olive oil, or as needed

MOJO SAUCE

3–4 tbsp extra virgin olive oil
8 garlic cloves, thinly sliced
250 ml tangerine juice
1/2 tsp ground cumin
black pepper to taste

NUTRITIONAL VALUES

1 To make the Mojo sauce, gently heat the olive oil with the sliced garlic until the garlic turns light golden (about 30 seconds), then add the remaining ingredients and remove from the heat. Leave to cool to room temperature, and taste for seasoning. This sauce keeps and stays delicious for about three days in the refrigerator.

2 Combine the tuna with the garlic, cumin, lime juice, black and cayenne pepper. Leave for about 30 minutes, then remove from the marinade and pat dry.

3 Brush the fish generously with olive oil, then cook quickly either in a frying pan or over a charcoal fire, about a minute or two on each side only.

4 Serve with the mojo sauce spooned over it when hot.

RABBIT WITH MUSTARD AND PRUNES

SERVES **4**

This risotto combines rabbit with a rich, sharp mustard and sweet juicy prunes.

450 g rabbit, diced
ground black pepper
2 tbsp wholegrain mustard
1 tbsp olive oil
1.1 litre chicken stock
6 shallots, quartered
400 g arborio rice
150 ml dry white wine
1 tbsp chopped fresh thyme or
1 tsp dried
75 g no-need-to-soak dried
prunes
fresh thyme, to garnish

1. Season the rabbit and coat with the mustard. Heat the oil in a large saucepan until sizzling, then fry the rabbit for 8–10 minutes all over until golden.

2. Meanwhile, pour the stock into a saucepan and bring to the boil. Reduce the heat to a gentle simmer.

3. Reduce the heat under the pan with the rabbit and gently fry the shallots for 2–3 minutes until just softened. Add the rice and cook, stirring, for 2 minutes until well coated in the rabbit juices.

4. Add the wine and thyme and cook gently, stirring, until absorbed. Ladle in the stock gradually until half is used, then add the prunes. Continue ladling in the stock until it is all absorbed and the rice is thick, creamy and tender. This will take about 25 minutes.

5. Adjust the seasoning and serve garnished with thyme.

NUTRITIONAL VALUES

VENISON WITH KUMQUATS AND WALNUTS

SERVES **4**

Kumquats have a sharp, citrus taste making them ideal to serve with rich game like venison. This is a truly impressive risotto.

8 x 75 g medallions of venison
ground black pepper
1 tbsp olive oil
100 g kumquats, sliced
1 tbsp caster sugar
1.1 litre beef stock
400 g arborio rice
65 g walnut pieces
1 tbsp walnut oil
4 tbsp snipped fresh chives
chives to garnish

1 Season the medallions lightly on both sides. Heat the olive oil in a frying pan until sizzling and fry the medallions over a moderate heat for 5–6 minutes on each side until cooked through. Remove from the pan, reserving the juices, and keep warm.

2 Meanwhile, place the kumquats in a saucepan with 100 ml water and the sugar. Bring to the boil and simmer for 2 minutes. Set aside to cool in the liquid.

3 Pour the stock into a saucepan and bring to the boil. Reduce the heat to a gentle simmer.

4 Transfer the reserved juices to a large saucepan and reheat. Add the rice and cook, stirring, for 2 minutes until well-coated in the juices.

5 Add a ladleful of stock and cook gently, stirring, until absorbed. Continue ladling the stock into the rice until all the liquid is absorbed and the rice becomes thick, creamy and tender. This will take about 25 minutes.

6 Stir in the kumquats and their cooking liquid until absorbed. Then add the walnut pieces, walnut oil and snipped chives. Adjust the seasoning and serve with the cooked venison.

NUTRITIONAL VALUES

MACKEREL AND ORANGE RISOTTO

SERVES **4**

Orange and mackerel are a classic combination, the oily fish being perfectly offset by the tangy citrus fruit.

900 ml fish stock
300 ml orange juice
2 tbsp olive oil
1 onion, finely chopped
2 garlic cloves, crushed
400 g arborio rice
ground black pepper
2 tsp fennel seeds
1 celery stalk, chopped
2 mackerel, cleaned, gutted and halved lengthways
2 oranges, peeled and sectioned
1 tbsp chopped fresh rosemary

NUTRITIONAL VALUES

1. Pour the stock and orange juice into a saucepan and bring to the boil. Reduce the heat to a gentle simmer.

2. Meanwhile, heat 1 tablespoon of olive oil in a large frying pan and gently cook the onion and half of the garlic for 2 minutes, stirring until the onion has softened but not browned. Stir in the rice and gently cook, stirring, for a further 2 minutes until well coated in oil.

3. Add a ladleful of stock and juice mixture and gently cook, stirring, until absorbed. Continue adding the stock and juice until half has been used. Season and add the fennel seeds and celery.

4. Continue adding the stock mixture until the rice is thick but not sticky, about 25 minutes. Meanwhile, brush the mackerel with the remaining garlic and oil and grill for 10 minutes, turning until cooked through. Remove as many bones as possible from the fish and cut the fish into large pieces. Gently stir into the rice with the orange sections and rosemary. Serve in a warm bowl.

POACHED SALMON FILLETS WITH DILL-AND-GINGER VINAIGRETTE

SERVES **4**

Salmon fillets are poached until tender in this easy recipe using a flavoured liquid including vinegar, dill and cloves.

4 boneless salmon fillets, 175 g each, with skin on
9 large sprigs fresh dill
1 bay leaf
4 whole cloves
9 whole black peppercorns
2 tbsp white wine vinegar

DILL-AND-GINGER VINAIGRETTE

2 tbsp French mustard
1 tbsp grated root ginger
2 tbsp finely chopped shallot
1 tsp finely chopped garlic
2 tbsp tarragon vinegar
50 g tinned pimentos, diced
freshly ground black pepper
125 ml olive oil

1 Prepare the vinaigrette by whisking the mustard, ginger, shallot, garlic, vinegar, pimentos and pepper together in a bowl. Then add the olive oil in a slow stream, whisking rapidly until well blended. Set aside.

2 Place the salmon fillets in a shallow saucepan with enough water to cover. Add all but one dill sprig, the bay leaves, cloves, peppercorns and vinegar. Bring the water to the boil and simmer for 3–5 minutes. Do not overcook. Drain and serve with the vinaigrette, giving the vinaigrette a last-second whisking, if necessary. Float the reserved sprig of dill on top of the bowl of vinaigrette.

NUTRITIONAL VALUES

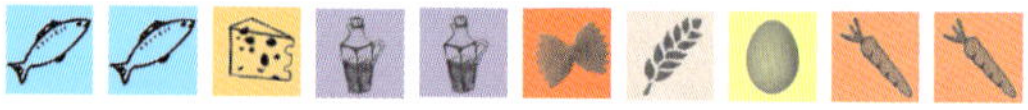

VENISON AND PRUNE STEW

SERVES **4**

A rich game meat that is naturally lean and low in fat. This beautiful combination of tender venison chunks cooked in red wine with assorted vegetables and soft prunes is delicious served with garlic-flavoured mashed potatoes.

675 g lean stewing venison, cut into 2.5 cm cubes
2 tbsp plain flour
salt substitute (see page 12)
black pepper
1 tsp dried mixed herbs
225 g shallots, peeled
2 large carrots, peeled and diced
2 stalks celery, trimmed and chopped
100 g mushrooms, wiped and halved
2 garlic cloves, peeled and minced
1 bouquet garni
237 ml dry red wine
237 ml fresh beef broth
2 tbsp redcurrant jelly
60 g no-soak dried prunes
2 tbsp chopped parsley, to garnish

1. Presoak the claypot. Place the venison in a bowl and add the flour, seasoning and mixed herbs. Toss well to coat the venison in the flour mixture.

2. Place the shallots, carrots, celery, mushrooms and garlic in the pot and mix well. Top with the venison, and push the bouquet garni into the vegetables. Pour over the red wine and broth and add the redcurrant jelly. Carefully mix well together. Top with the prunes and season well. Cover and place in a cold oven. Set the oven to 200°C/gas mark 6 and cook for 2 hours. Remove the lid and cook, uncovered, for a further 10 minutes.

3. Serve the venison on warmed serving plates, sprinkled with chopped parsley.

NUTRITIONAL VALUES

GRILLED SHARK STEAKS WITH CITRUS SALSA

SERVES **4**

Served with the refreshing flavour of citrus salsa, these shark steaks make a very interesting main course.

2 medium oranges
1 small red onion, chopped
1 garlic clove, peeled and crushed
1–2 fresh green chillies, roasted, peeled, seeded and coarsely chopped
1 tbsp olive oil
3 tbsp freshly squeezed lime juice
2 tbsp chopped coriander leaves
salt substitute (see page 12)
freshly ground black pepper

SHARK STEAKS

4 x 9.5 cm thick shark, tuna or swordfish steaks (175–225 g each)
4 tsp olive oil
salt substitute (see page 12)
freshly ground black pepper

1 Peel the oranges over a small bowl with a vegetable knife, cutting through the peel and just barely into the flesh, then spiralling down and around from one end to the other, as if peeling an apple. Cut into the flesh next to each dividing membrane and pop out each segment, removing any pips. Reserve.

2 In the bowl of a food processor or blender, process the remaining salsa ingredients, pulsing on and off and scraping down the sides of the bowl until well chopped. Add the oranges and continue processing until you have a chunky, well-combined mixture. Cover and set aside at room temperature for 1 hour.

3 Brush the shark steaks on both sides with oil, and sprinkle with the salt substitute and pepper to taste. Grill under a medium heat for 4–5 minutes on each side, or until the fish feels firm but bouncy. Serve immediately with the salsa.

NUTRITIONAL VALUES

STEAMED PRAWNS WITH CRANBERRY GAZPACHO

SERVES **2**

CRANBERRY GAZPACHO

1 small cucumber

1 red pepper, cored and seeded

½ green pepper, cored and seeded

1 mild green chilli, seeded

2 large ripe tomatoes

4 spring onions

1 bunch parsley

1 tbsp lemon juice or wine vinegar

salt substitute (see page 12)

250 ml water

scant 50 g fresh cranberries

1. To make the cranberry gazpacho, very finely chop the cucumber, peppers, chilli, tomatoes, spring onions and parsley. Combine in a large bowl.
2. Add lemon juice, salt substitute and pepper. Set aside.
3. In a 1 litre saucepan, bring the water to the boil. Cook the cranberries for about 1 minute, or until a few cranberries split. Allow the cranberries to cool. When cool, add them to the gazpacho. Cover and refrigerate.

4 tbsp cranberry gazpacho

425 ml water

100 g basmati rice

freshly ground black pepper

12 large raw prawns

4 tbsp very finely chopped parsley

1. Prepare the cranberry gazpacho and set aside.
2. In a small saucepan, bring to the boil 175 ml water. Add the rice and lower the heat. Stir, while adding pepper. Cover and cook for 12–15 minutes, until all the liquid is absorbed. Set aside.
3. In a small saucepan on medium heat, heat the cranberry gazpacho. Add 2 tablespoons of water and cook until the water is evaporated. Set aside.
4. In a deep saucepan, bring to the boil 250 ml water. Place the prawns in a strainer and place the strainer in the saucepan. Cover and cook for about 3–4 minutes, or until prawns are firm and opaque. Drain and set aside.
5. Toss the parsley with rice, and arrange on plates.
6. Place the cranberry gazpacho on the rice and arrange the prawns on plates.

NUTRITIONAL VALUES

CHICKEN WITH 40 CLOVES OF GARLIC

SERVES **4**

Although 40 cloves of garlic may sound like a huge quantity, they are roasted in their skins and impart the most delicious flavour to this famous French dish from Dauphine.

large bunch of parsley, thyme and rosemary

2 bay leaves

1 whole chicken, weighing approx. 1.75 kg

salt substitute (see page 12)

freshly ground black pepper

7 tbsp olive oil

40 garlic cloves, unpeeled

90 g plain flour

5 tbsp water

1 Preheat the oven to 180°C/Gas mark 4. Form the herbs into two bouquet garnis, one slightly smaller than the other.

NUTRITIONAL VALUES

2 Wash and pat dry the chicken and season inside and out with the salt substitute and pepper. Place the smaller bouquet garni in the cavity of the chicken. Pour the oil into a casserole which is large enough to hold the chicken with the lid on, and add the second bouquet garni and the garlic cloves.

3 Gently heat the oil on the hob. Add the chicken and turn it to coat it in oil, ensuring the herbs remain beneath the chicken.

4 Mix the flour and water to form a thick paste. Roll the paste into a long rope shape and place this around the edge of the casserole to act as a seal for the lid. Roast in the oven for 1½ hours.

5 To serve, either break and clean off the seal before taking the dish to the table or break the seal in front of your guests, filling the room with a delicious aroma. Serve with new potatoes, broccoli or green salad.

TROUT IN TOMATO SAUCE

SERVES **4**

Wonderfully fresh and tender young trout are a real joy to eat. Choose smallish trout that do not have thick skins.

28 g parsley

1 garlic clove, chopped

3 tbsp olive oil

560 g well-flavoured tomatoes, skinned, seeded and chopped

½ tsp tomato purée

salt substitute (see page 12)

4 trout, about 198 g

1. Fry the parsley and garlic in the oil in a pan large enough to hold the fish in a single layer, for 1–2 minutes. Stir in the tomatoes and tomato purée and simmer for 5 minutes.
2. Season the sauce, add the trout, and spoon some of the sauce over them to half-cover. Cover and cook gently for about 20 minutes.
3. Serve with crusty granary bread.

NUTRITIONAL VALUES

WHITE CHILLI WITH CHICKEN

SERVES **6**

This is a low-fat, moderately spicy chilli, made with a delicious combination of chicken, white beans and chillies.

- 350 g white beans, picked over and soaked overnight
- 1 tbsp chilli powder
- ½ tsp ground cumin
- ½ tsp dried thyme
- ½ tsp dried oregano
- ½ tsp cayenne pepper
- ½ tsp garlic powder
- 1 tbsp plain flour
- 3 chicken half-breasts, cut into 12 mm cubes
- 2 tbsp olive oil
- 1 onion, chopped
- 1 celery stick, chopped
- 450 ml chicken stock
- 4 chillies, roasted, peeled and chopped, or 100 g tin chopped green chillies
- about 1 tsp salt substitute (see page 12)
- 15 g fresh coriander, chopped

1. Drain the beans, put them in a large pan and barely cover with fresh water. Bring to the boil, reduce heat and simmer.
2. Mix the spices, herbs, seasonings and flour. Toss the spice mix with the cubed chicken so the meat is evenly coated with spices, and set aside.
3. Heat 1 tablespoon of the olive oil in a frying pan and sauté the onion and celery for 6 minutes. Add the vegetables to the beans.
4. Heat the remaining olive oil in a frying pan and cook the chicken, turning often, until all sides are lightly browned. Add the chicken to the beans with the chicken stock and chillies. Simmer until the beans are tender, about 1½ hours in total, adding water or chicken stock if needed.
5. Add salt to taste and adjust seasonings. Add the coriander just before serving.

NUTRITIONAL VALUES

STRETCH-YOUR-BEEF CHILLI BEANS

SERVES **6**

This economical chilli uses only a small amount of beef, with kidney beans and lots of vegetables giving it substance. It is a thick, hot chilli, but can be made milder by removing the veins and seeds from the jalapeños.

175 g dried kidney beans, picked over and soaked overnight
3 tbsp vegetable oil
350 g beef, cut into 5 mm dice
1½ onions
2 celery stalks, chopped
1 small green pepper, diced
4 garlic cloves, minced
425 g tin tomatoes, chopped
250 ml tin tomato sauce
3 jalapeño chillies, unseeded, minced
1 tsp ground cumin
1 tsp dried oregano
1 tsp paprika
½ tsp ground coriander
2–3 beef stock cubes, crumbled

1 Drain the kidney beans, put them in a large pan and cover with water. Bring to the boil, reduce heat and simmer.

2 Heat 1 tablespoon of the olive oil in a frying pan and brown the meat. Add the meat to the beans, discarding fat. Heat the remaining 2 tablespoons of the olive oil in the pan and sauté the onion, celery, green pepper and garlic for 5 minutes. Add the vegetables to the beans. Add the remaining ingredients. Bring to the boil, reduce heat and simmer for at least 1½ hours, adding water if needed.

NUTRITIONAL VALUES

BAKED TROUT WITH POMEGRANATE

SERVES **4**

Pomegranates are one of the many exotic fruits which are now readily available and make a wonderful accompaniment to this nutritious fish.

1 large ripe pomegranate
1 tbsp olive oil
1 onion, finely chopped
2 garlic cloves, peeled and finely chopped
125 g pecans, coarsely chopped
4 tbsp chopped fresh parsley
freshly ground black pepper
¼ tsp ground cardamom
2 tbsp wine vinegar
2 tbsp olive oil
4 trout, 300–375 g each, cleaned and dressed
curly kale for garnish

1 With a sharp knife, cut the top off the pomegranate. Score fruit in about 6 wedges and pull apart into separate sections. Gently scoop the seeds into a small bowl. Set aside.

2 In a medium frying pan, over medium–high heat, heat the olive oil. Add onion and cook until softened and beginning to color, 3 to 5 minutes. Add garlic and cook 1 minute longer.

3 Stir in pecans, parsley and black pepper to taste, cardamom, vinegar and half the olive oil. Remove from heat. Stir in three-quarters of the pomegranate seeds.

4 Preheat oven to 200°C/gas mark 6. Lightly grease a large shallow baking dish. Rinse fish under cold running water and pat dry with paper towels. Score each fish in two places on each side. Spoon one-quarter of the onion mixture into each fish.

5 Arrange the fish in baking dish, drizzle with remaining olive oil and bake, uncovered, until the flesh flakes easily if tested with the tip of a knife, 12-15 minutes. Serve fish on a bed of curly kale and sprinkle with pomegranate seeds.

NUTRITIONAL VALUES

SHREDDED BEEF WITH CELERY

SERVES **4 - 6**

This recipe is a wonderful example of Chinese cooking. The celery and ginger help to give it a clean, refreshing taste.

225 g beef steak

50 g celery

50 g leek and scallion

2 slices fresh root ginger

1 tbsp chilli paste

2 tbsp soy sauce

1 tbsp rice wine or dry sherry

1 tsp vinegar

3 tbsp oil

1 Shred the beef into thin matchstick-sized strips. Shred the celery and leeks to the same size (Chinese leeks are a cross between the Western leek and spring onion with the skin and green foliage). Peel the root ginger and cut it into thin shreds.

2 Heat up the wok or pan and put in the oil. When it starts to smoke, stir-fry the beef for a short while, add the celery, leek and ginger root, followed by the soy sauce and wine. Stir for 1–2 minutes, then add vinegar and serve.

Celery is low in saturated fat and very low in cholesterol and makes an ideal stir-fry vegetable.

NUTRITIONAL VALUES

TUNA STEAKS WITH PEPPER SAUCE

SERVES **4**

Tuna is a very 'meaty' fish with a texture similar to tender beef. It is ideal for grilling or barbecuing and here it is seasoned with mustard, paprika and cayenne pepper before cooking. It is served with a tangy pepper sauce that is flavoured with harissa, a fragrant chilli sauce from North Africa.

4 fresh tuna steaks, each weighing about 250 g
freshly ground black pepper
4 tbsp Dijon mustard
2 tbsp dry white wine
1 tsp paprika pepper
1/2 tsp cayenne pepper
2 tbsp olive oil
lime wedges, to serve

PEPPER SAUCE

3 tbsp olive oil
250 g shallots, sliced
2 garlic cloves, finely chopped
2 tsp harissa
2 red peppers, deseeded and sliced
400 g tin of chopped tomatoes
150 ml dry white wine
60 g pitted black olives, sliced

1 Wash and pat dry the tuna steaks. Season with pepper on both sides. Mix the mustard, wine and spices and spread over both sides of the tuna. Put in a shallow dish, cover and chill for an hour.

2 Meanwhile, make the sauce. Heat the oil in a saucepan and gently fry the shallots, garlic, harissa and red peppers for 5 minutes, bring to the boil, and leave to simmer for 30 minutes, until thick and pulpy. Season and stir in the olives. Set aside.

3 Preheat the grill to medium. Put the tuna steaks in a foil-lined grill pan. Drizzle with a little olive oil and cook for 5–6 minutes on each side, until golden and cooked through to your liking. Drain and garnish with wedges of lime and the sauce, serve hot or cold.

NUTRITIONAL VALUES

SPICE-CRUSTED TUNA WITH VEGETABLES AND TOFU

SERVES **4**

Cooking time for the tuna will depend on how thick the steaks are and how rare you like your fish – allow 1–2 minutes a side over a fairly brisk heat.

4 tuna steaks

2 tbsp coriander seeds, finely crushed

1 tsp chilli sauce

2 tsp fresh ginger purée

250 g green beans, trimmed

125 g asparagus spears

1 bunch of spring onions, trimmed

3 tbsp olive oil

250 g firm tofu, cut into sticks measuring roughly 4 x 1 cm

juice of 2 limes

4 sprigs fresh coriander

4 tbsp chopped fresh parsley

1. Place the tuna steaks side by side in a shallow dish. Mix together the crushed coriander, chilli and ginger, and spread over the fish.

2. Heat a ridged grill pan until very hot, then add the olive oil. When foaming, add the tuna steaks, spiced sides down, with any juices from the dish. Sauté for 1–2 minutes, turn over, and continue to cook for 1–2 minutes or until done to your liking. Drain from the pan and keep warm with the vegetables.

3. Add the tofu and sauté for 2–3 minutes until heated through, then squeeze in the lime juice. Arrange the vegetables and tofu on serving plates with the tuna steaks on top. Stir the pan juices briefly and spoon over the steaks. Tuck a few coriander leaves amongst the vegetables and tofu, and scatter the parsley over the tuna.

NUTRITIONAL VALUES

TUNA TOFU NIÇOISE

SERVES **4**

Grill the tuna and tofu conventionally or cook in a ridged griddle pan. Make sure the pan is really hot before adding a little olive oil and then the fish and tofu. If the food sticks initially, leave it to cook over a high heat for a minute or two, by which time it will have sealed and released itself from the pan.

100 g green beans
100 ml olive oil
4 tbsp lemon juice
freshly ground black pepper
1 tbsp chopped fresh oregano
12 baby plum tomatoes, cut into halves
1 red onion, peeled and finely chopped
75 g cucumber, sliced
50 g black olives
250 g fresh tuna steak
250 g firm tofu
lemon wedges, to garnish

1 Cook the green beans in a pan of boiling water for 2 minutes. Drain and refresh by running cold water over them.

2 Reserve 1 tablespoon olive oil and put the rest in a large bowl with the lemon juice, pepper and oregano. Whisk together until combined, then add the beans, tomato halves, chopped onion, cucumber and olives. Toss lightly to coat with the dressing, then set aside.

3 Slice the tuna and tofu into 5 cm strips and season. Heat a ridged griddle pan and, when really hot, add the reserved olive oil. Cook the tuna and tofu in batches for 1–2 minutes on each side, depending on thickness. If using a conventional grill, preheat it to high, brush the tuna and tofu with the oil, and place on a foil-lined rack. Cook as close to the heat as possible.

4 Spoon the bean salad on to serving plates and serve with the hot tuna and tofu. Pour over any dressing left in the bowl and garnish with lemon wedges.

NUTRITIONAL VALUES

FRESH TUNA BRAISED BORDELAIS STYLE

SERVES **4**

This is one of the most delicious ways to cook tuna. The combination of onions, tomatoes and mushrooms really complements the fish.

- 6 tbsp olive oil
- 450 g fresh tuna
- 1 large onion
- 5 medium tomatoes
- 150 ml white wine
- 150 ml fish stock
- 225 g mushrooms
- pepper to taste

NUTRITIONAL VALUES

1 Heat 4 tablespoons of the olive oil over a medium heat. Brown the fish in the oil on both sides – about 2 minutes per side. Thinly slice the onion and add to the fish.

2 As the onion is cooking, deseed then dice the tomatoes. Add them to the mixture, together with the white wine and the fish stock. Bring the liquid to the boil, then lower the heat to a gentle simmer.

3 Cook the fish for 15 minutes, retrieve from the pan juices and set aside to keep warm.

4 With the remaining 2 tablespoons of olive oil, fry the mushrooms until golden and add them to the pan juices. Turn up the heat and reduce by one-third. When the liquor is reduced, check the seasoning, pour over the tuna and serve immediately with boiled new potatoes.

AUBERGINE AND SWEET POTATO CURRY

SERVES **4**

This makes a very substantial main course, but could also be served as a side dish to accompany meat or fish curries.

2 tbsp cumin seeds
1 tbsp mustard seeds
3 tbsp olive oil
2 small sweet potatoes, about 450 g, peeled and cut into 2.5 cm chunks
1 large onion, finely sliced
2 garlic cloves, finely sliced
1–2 tsp chilli powder
1 tsp ground turmeric
1 large aubergine, cut to the same size as the potato
1 tbsp blue poppy seeds
240 ml water or vegetable broth
2 tsp salt substitute (see page 12)
1 tbsp torn fresh coriander leaves

1 Heat a large frying pan over a medium heat, then add the cumin and mustard seeds and dry-fry for 30 seconds or so, until aromatic and starting to pop. Transfer to a plate and leave to cool.

2 Heat the olive oil in the pan, add the potatoes and cook for 3–4 minutes until starting to soften. Add the onion, garlic, chilli powder and turmeric and cook for 1–2 minutes, then add the aubergine with the roasted spices and the poppy seeds. Stir in the water and salt substitute, then cover and simmer very slowly for 30–45 minutes, until the vegetables are tender.

3 Season the curry to taste, then serve sprinkled with the coriander.

NUTRITIONAL VALUES

GRILLED SARDINES WITH SPAGHETTI SQUASH

SERVES **4**

Really fresh sardines have a delicious flavour which doesn't want to be challenged by anything else, so serving it with a mild-tasting spaghetti squash is both simple and delicious.

1 small spaghetti squash (weighing about 735 g), peeled, deseeded and diced
2 tbsp extra virgin olive oil
12 fresh sardines, scaled
2 large tomatoes, deseeded and diced
12 black olives, pitted and diced
freshly ground black pepper
green salad, to serve

NUTRITIONAL VALUES

1. Preheat the grill. Cook the diced squash in the olive oil for 3–4 minutes, stirring frequently, while grilling the sardines for 2–3 minutes on each side. Brush the fish with a little oil before cooking, just to stop them sticking to the grill rack or pan.

2. Toss the tomatoes and olives into the pan with the squash and just heat through. Season well, then pile the squash mixture onto warmed serving plates. Add the grilled sardines and a little green salad, and serve immediately.

TURKEY CHILLI WITH GREEN CHILLIES

SERVES **6**

Turkey can provide a lower-cholesterol alternative to traditional beef and pork chillies. This is a substantial chilli with a savoury, moderately spicy sauce. It is made from mild green Anaheim chillies, and the heat is provided by cayenne pepper, but other green chillies can be substituted.

6 large Anaheim chillies
1 tbsp olive oil
675 g uncooked turkey meat, cubed
1 medium onion, chopped
1 celery stalk, finely chopped
2 garlic cloves, minced
750 ml chicken stock
425 g tin tomatoes
½ tsp cayenne or to taste
425 g tin white or kidney beans

1 Roast the chillies under a grill, turning, until skin on all sides is blistered and mostly blackened. Put the chillies in a paper bag or covered bowl to steam.

2 Heat the olive oil in a large frying pan, add the turkey meat and cook until browned. Add the onion, celery and garlic, and cook for 5 minutes. Put the meat and vegetables in a large saucepan with the chicken stock. Bring to the boil, reduce heat and simmer.

3 Peel the blackened skins from the chillies and remove the stems and seeds. Chop half the chillies and add to the stew. Cut the three remaining chillies in several large pieces. Put the chillies and tomatoes in a blender or food processor with as much of the tomato liquid as is needed and purée. Add the tomato-chilli purée, and any remaining tomato liquid, to the chilli. Add the cayenne.

4 When the chilli has simmered at least 45 minutes, add the beans and cook for 5 minutes. Taste and adjust seasoning if desired.

NUTRITIONAL VALUES

FRESH CHICKEN WITH LEMON GRASS AND CASHEW NUTS

SERVES **4**

The cashew nuts really add crunch and flavour to this declicious Far Eastern recipe.

Olive oil

2 small dried chillies

1 clove garlic, chopped

450 g lean, corn-fed chicken, sliced

½ tsp sugar

1 tbsp oyster sauce

1 tbsp fish sauce or light soy sauce

3 tbsp chicken stock or water

50 g roasted, unsalted cashew nuts

1 tbsp chopped lemon grass

2 shallots, cut in quarters

1 With a drop or two of olive oil, stir-fry the chillies until cooked evenly but not firm. Set aside.

2 Stir-fry the garlic with a few more drops of olive oil until golden. Add the chicken slices, sugar and oyster and fish sauces and stir-fry until the chicken is golden in colour. Lower the heat and add the stock. Cook for a few more minutes, stirring occasionally.

3 When the chicken is thoroughly cooked, add the cashew nuts, lemon grass, shallots and chillies, and stir several times, being careful not to break the chillies. Remove from the heat and serve.

NUTRITIONAL VALUES

CHICKEN WITH SPINACH OR BROCCOLI

SERVES **4**

A mainstay of home cooking, this dish pleases everyone in the family. A handful of fresh fenugreek leaves lends a unique, appetizing fragrance to the dish, so do use them if you are able to.

450 g chicken breast
450 g fresh spinach or broccoli
1 tbsp ginger and garlic paste
50 g fenugreek leaves (optional)
50 g onion, chopped
1 tsp chilli powder
¼ tsp turmeric
½ tsp garam masala
½ tsp cumin seeds, crushed
2 tbsp olive oil
1½ tbsp low-fat natural yoghurt
1 green chilli

1 Wash and skin the chicken and cut into 2.5 cm cubes.

2 Wash the spinach in plenty of running water, carefully removing all the grit, then drain it well.

3 Roughly chop the leaves, discarding the stalks.

4 Pour 115 ml of water into a medium-sized heavy saucepan. Add the ginger and garlic paste, the onion, chilli powder, turmeric, garam masala and cumin seeds. Bring it to the boil, cover and simmer for 3–4 minutes.

5 Drop the chicken pieces into the pan and simmer, uncovered, for 15–20 minutes, or until most of the moisture has evaporated.

6 Add the olive oil and cook over a higher heat, stirring continuously, until the food looks slightly glazed.

7 Add the yoghurt, spinach or broccoli, with the fenugreek and green chilli, blending everything well so that the spices coat the spinach evenly. Cover and cook over a low heat for about 10 minutes, or until the spinach releases its own moisture. Remove the lid and simmer uncovered. It is important to note that the dish is not ready if it still looks a little watery. The finished dish must be almost dry with a hint of sheen to it.

GINGER AND GARLIC PASTE

To make the ginger and garlic paste is simplicity itself. You will need 115 g fresh ginger, lightly scraped, washed and cut into chunks, and the same amount of fresh garlic, peeled. Put all the ingredients into a blender with a very little water, just sufficient to facilitate the grinding process.

Spoon the paste into an airtight jar and store it on the bottom shelf of the fridge. It will keep for 2–3 weeks, or alternatively you can freeze it.

NUTRITIONAL VALUES

BRAISED SWORDFISH WITH PEPPERS

SERVES **4**

A red pepper is one of the healthiest vegetables you can eat. It's a great source of vitamin C and also contains carotenoid beta-carotene.

4 swordfish steaks (about 170 g each)
4 tbsp olive oil
4 cloves garlic
1 medium onion, roughly chopped
1 medium red pepper
110 g fresh or tinned plum tomatoes, roughly chopped
1 chilli pepper
158 ml dry white wine
salt substitute (see page 12) and pepper to taste

NUTRITIONAL VALUES

1 Wash and thoroughly dry the steaks. Heat the oil over a high heat and seal each steak on each side.

2 Remove the fish from the pan and reserve it. Turn down the heat to medium and add the whole cloves of garlic and the onions.

3 Turn the heat once more to high and cook the onions until the edges begin to catch. Reduce the flame to a gentle simmer and cook on until the onions and garlic are softened. In the meantime, deseed and finely slice the peppers.

4 When the onions are soft, add the peppers and cook until they begin to soften – about 5 minutes. Add the tomatoes, the whole chilli and the wine. Bring to a fierce boil, then add the fish. Turn the heat to a low simmer and cover the pan. Simmer until the fish is very tender – about 15 minutes.

5 Remove the fish from the pan and set it aside in a warm place. Boil up the pan juices very briskly, until they are reduced to a thick, creamy mixture. Season, pour around the fish and serve.

RABBIT WITH ONIONS

SERVES **4**

Onions don't just add flavour to a dish but are also a great source of phytochemicals and nutrients.

1 large rabbit (weighing about 900 g)
4 tbsp vegetable oil
3 large onions
6 cloves garlic
6 bay leaves
3 chilli peppers
4 good sprigs fresh rosemary
4 tbsp brandy
salt subtitute (see page 12) and freshly ground black pepper to taste

NUTRITIONAL VALUES

1 Preheat the oven to 180°C/gas mark 4. Cut away the legs from the rabbit carcase and joint each one once more at the knee. Cut the saddle into four pieces: haunch, belly and the rib cage, split in two along the breast bone.

2 Heat the oil over a medium heat and brown the rabbit pieces for 3–4 minutes. Remove them from the pan with a slotted spoon and set aside.

3 Slice the onions very finely and add them to the rabbit pan. Increase the heat and cook them until they begin to colour. Reduce the heat and add the whole garlic, the whole chillies and the whole sprigs of rosemary.

4 Return the rabbit to the pan and smother with the onions. Cover tightly and put them in the oven.

5 After about 1 hour, completely turn all the contents, add the brandy and season. Continue cooking until the rabbit is very tender – another 30 minutes or so.

RABBIT CASSEROLED IN RED WINE

SERVES **6**

Rabbit meat is very flavourful but has no fat, so it is ideal in healthy diets.

3 tbsp olive oil
1 rabbit, weighing about 1.7 kg
40 g plain flour
2 garlic cloves, minced
1 large onion, finely minced
450 ml red wine
5 slices of lean bacon
20 small onions
450 g new potatoes
salt substitute (see page 12) and freshly ground black pepper

NUTRITIONAL VALUES

1 Preheat the oven to 160°C/gas mark 3. Cut up the rabbit and brown in half of the olive oil for about 5 minutes. Sprinkle the browning pieces with the flour, the crushed garlic and the finely chopped onion. Add the red wine and enough water to cover the meat. Braise the rabbit, covered, in a warm oven.

2 While the rabbit is cooking, dice the bacon and peel the small onions. Brown them both in the remaining olive oil. Set aside.

3 After 20 minutes, add the bacon and onions to the rabbit. Re-cover.

4 As the rabbit, bacon and onions are cooking, peel the new potatoes. After a further 20 minutes add these to the rabbit.

5 Cook the casserole for another hour or so, season and serve.

MOROCCAN CHICKEN

SERVES **4**

The lemon used in this recipe permeates the chicken, and olives add piquancy to the flavour. Try combinations of different olives for variety.

1 chicken, cut into serving pieces
1 tbsp cumin
½ tsp ginger
½ tsp paprika
5 garlic cloves, chopped
several handfuls of fresh coriander, chopped
juice of 2 lemons
ground black and cayenne pepper, to taste
3-5 tbsp flour
4 tomatoes, chopped (either fresh or tinned)
10-15 each (three types in total) of your chosen olives
1 lemon, cut into 6 wedges
4 tbsp extra virgin olive oil
235 ml chicken stock
extra lemon juice, to taste

1 Combine the chicken with cumin, paprika, ginger, turmeric, garlic, coriander, lemon juice and pepper. Place in a baking dish in a single layer. Leave to marinate for 30 minutes, then add the flour. Toss the ingredients together to coat well.

2 Preheat the oven to 160°C/gas mark 3. Add the tomatoes, olives, lemon wedges, olive oil and stock to the dish. Bake uncovered for about an hour, or until the chicken is tender and a delicious sauce has formed. Add extra lemon juice, if desired.

NUTRITIONAL VALUES

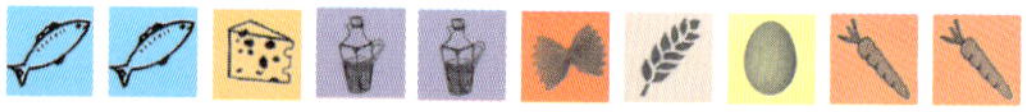

MALTAGLIATI WITH LAMB & CHIVES

SERVES **4**

Any ribbon-like pasta works well in this recipe as it coats easily with the sauce. Serve sprinkled with Parmesan cheese and chives.

3 tbsp olive oil

2 garlic cloves, peeled and finely chopped

1 large onion, peeled and chopped

280 g lean lamb, trimmed and finely chopped

400 g tin chopped tomatoes

1 tbsp tomatoe purée

4 tbsp red wine

1 tbsp snipped chives

salt substitute (see page 12)

freshly ground black pepper

450 g fresh maltagliati

2–3 tbsp freshly grated Parmesan cheese and extra snipped chives, to serve

1 Heat the oil in a heavy saucepan and sauté the garlic and onion for 5 minutes or until softened. Add the lamb and continue to sauté for 5 minutes, stirring frequently, until browned.

2 Add the tomatoes, tomato purée blended with 2 tablespoons water and the wine. Bring to the boil, reduce the heat, cover with a lid and let simmer for 40 minutes or until a thick sauce is formed. Add the chives and season to taste. Continue to simmer for 5 minutes while cooking the pasta.

3 Cook the pasta in plenty of salted boiling water for 1–2 minutes or until firm to bite. Drain and return to the pan. Add the sauce, toss lightly and serve.

NUTRITIONAL VALUES

GARLIC MACKEREL WITH SHARP GOOSEBERRY SAUCE

SERVES **4**

The garlic and oily fish make this a great healthy dish with huge amounts of flavour.

2 large, fresh mackerel
2 small lemons
3 cloves of garlic, peeled
2 tbsp oil
salt substitute (see page 12)
freshly ground black pepper
350 g sharp, green gooseberries
a little sugar (optional)

1 Wash and gut the mackerel, and cut three or four diagonal slashes down the side of each fish.

2 Cut one of the lemons and one of the garlic cloves into four slices, and put two pieces on each fish.

3 Juice the remaining lemon, crush the rest of the garlic and combine with the oil, a little salt and plenty of black pepper, and pour over the fish.

4 Leave the mackerel to marinate in a cool place for 2-4 hours.

5 To make the sauce, top and tail (trim) the gooseberries and cook in a covered pan with a little water over a low heat until tender. Add sugar to taste and sieve the fruit.

6 To cook the mackerel, drain off the marinade and grill under a moderate heat for 20-25 minutes, turning once and basting from time to time with the marinade.

NUTRITIONAL VALUES

CHINESE-STYLE SEA BASS WITH GINGER

SERVES **4**

Sea bass has an exquisite flavour and is an ideal fish to grill whole. Take the whole fish to the table for an impressive centrepiece. It is simple to serve as the flesh comes away easily and there are very few bones to worry about.

1 tbsp sesame oil

1 sea bass, weighing 1–1.25 kg, gutted, scaled and with the gills removed

2 or 3 garlic cloves, finely sliced

2.5 cm piece of fresh root ginger, peeled and thinly sliced

3 tbsp light soy sauce

2 tbsp rice-wine vinegar

4 spring onions, thinly shredded

1 Preheat the grill to high. Line a grill pan with foil and brush it with some of the oil. Wash and pat dry the sea bass and make four deep incisions diagonally across both sides. Put the sea bass in the grill pan and insert half the slices of garlic and ginger into the stomach cavity. Put a slice of ginger or garlic in each slit. Combine the soy sauce and vinegar and pour half over the fish. Position the grill pan about 10 cm away from the heat and grill the fish for about 10-12 minutes, occasionally brushing it with oil and basting it with the soy sauce and vinegar.

2 Turn the fish over, put the remaining ginger and garlic in the slits and pour over the remaining soy sauce mixture. Grill for a further 10-12 minutes. Turning the fish over without breaking it can be quite tricky, so use a couple of fish slices or long serving implements.

3 Once cooked, carefully remove the fish to a warmed serving platter and scatter the shredded spring onions on and around it. Serve immediately, accompanied by noodles or rice and stir-fried vegetables.

NUTRITIONAL VALUES

TROUT WITH ALMONDS

SERVES **4**

This trout with almonds dish is a delicious way to help your heart. Trout is a great source of omega–3 oils, and almonds and soy have been proven to reduce your body's cholesterol.

4 trout, cleaned
4 tbsp milk
2 tbsp seasoned flour
4 tbsp olive oil
6 tsp flaked almonds
4 sprigs parsley
4 sprigs watercress

NUTRITIONAL VALUES

1 Dip the trout in seasoned milk and then into the flour.

2 Heat 2 tablespoons olive oil in a frying pan and lightly fry the almonds. Shake and turn the almonds to brown evenly. Remove and keep warm.

3 Heat the remaining olive oil and shallow fry the trout on both sides for about 4 minutes each side. Arrange the almonds on top of the trout during the last 2 minutes of cooking. Alternatively, remove the top skin showing the pink flesh after cooking and arrange the almonds on top and re-heat for a few minutes under the grill.

4 Replace the fish eye with a sprig of parsley or watercress.

RABBIT FLORENTINE

SERVES **4**

Pieces of tender young rabbit – a low-fat choice for a dinner party or family meal – are served on a bed of orange-flavoured spinach. You could substitute sorrel, which has an even more pronounced citrus flavour.

1 kg rabbit pieces, trimmed, wiped and dried
juice of 1 orange
salt substitute (see page 12)
freshly ground black pepper
2 tsp dried oregano
olive oil
675 g spinach, stalks removed, washed and drained
juice of ½ orange
1 tsp grated orange rind
large pinch ground coriander
150 ml low-fat yoghurt
2 tbsp chopped hazelnuts
orange slices

NUTRITIONAL VALUES

1 Set the oven to 190°C/gas mark 5. Sprinkle the rabbit with orange juice, season with salt substitute and pepper and sprinkle on the oregano. Place the rabbit in a lightly-oiled baking dish, cover with foil and bake in the oven for about 1½ hours, or until the meat is tender. Turn the rabbit joints once or twice during cooking.

2 Just before the rabbit is done, make the spinach layer. Cook the leaves in a large pan without added water over medium heat for 3 minutes, or until they collapse. Turn them into a colander and drain thoroughly, pressing out all the moisture.

3 Return the spinach to the dry pan and stir in the orange juice and rind, ground coriander and yoghurt. Season with salt substitute and pepper and heat gently.

4 Turn the spinach onto a heated serving dish and arrange the rabbit pieces on top. Sprinkle on chopped hazlenuts, and garnish with orange slices. Potatoes boiled in their jackets, or whole-wheat noodles are good accompaniments.

Spinach is rich in vitamins and minerals, particularly folic acid, vitamin K, magnesium, and manganese; it also contains more protein than most vegetables.

CHICKEN PACKETS WITH SPRING VEGETABLES

SERVES **6**

This is the simplest and heathiest dish you can imagine, but the contents of the foil packets must be thoroughly cooked through. Never put too many in your oven, and keep them all in the centre. Chicken is tender enough to be ideal for this method, and the vegetables will retain all of their natural goodness.

3 chicken breasts, skinned and boned
200 g snow peas
200 g green beans, sliced in thirds crosswise
200 g carrots, cut into matchstick strips
3 celery stalks, cut into matchstick strips
3 courgettes, cut into small rounds
1 tbsp chopped mixed herbs
1 tbsp salt substitute (see page 12)

NUTRITIONAL VALUES

1. Cut the chicken breasts into bite-sized pieces. Trim the snow peas. Mix all the vegetables together and sprinkle them with mixed herbs and salt substitute.
2. Lay a sheet of foil on a work surface. Cut it into 15 cm wide strips. Cut the strips into pieces 20 cm long.
3. Arrange 2 chicken pieces and a tablespoon of vegetables in the centre of each foil rectangle. Fold the strip over the top, then fold the edges over several times to seal the contents. You should have about 20 packets.
4. Put them into a preheated 180°C/gas mark 4 oven and cook for 30 minutes. Check one of the packets, opening it carefully as a lot of steam will escape. If it is done, you can serve the packets. Let the diners unwrap them for themselves.

SIMMERED MACKEREL IN MISO SAUCE

SERVES **2**

This dish is a particular favourite in autumn, when the mackerel is reputed to be best. The mackerel is cooked unboned to give extra flavour.

450 g mackerel, head removed and gutted

100 ml water

2 tbsp caster sugar

1 tbsp sake

50 g miso

1 thin slice peeled root ginger

2 spring onions, cut in half

NUTRITIONAL VALUES

1 Cut the mackerel in half close to one side of the backbone to make 2 pieces of fish, one with the backbone attached and one without. Cut each piece in half again.

2 Put the water, sugar, sake and miso in a pan then heat until the liquid is simmering. Add the fish and ginger and continue to simmer, covered, for 7–8 minutes with a lid, slightly smaller than the pan and placed directly onto the fish. Use aluminium foil if you do not have a lid.

3 Add the spring onions and simmer for a further 5–10 minutes. Serve immediately with the rice and a vegetable dish.

Ginger helps to stimulate the gastric juices and can be found fresh in the produce section of most grocery stores. Look for smooth skin with a fresh, spicy fragrance. Tubers should be firm and feel heavy. Length is a sign of maturity, and mature rhizomes will be hotter and more fibrous. Avoid those with wrinkled flesh, as this is an indication of aged ginger past its prime.

KATSUO TATAKI

SERVES **4**

Katsuo is the Japanese word for 'bonito', a close relative of the Mediterranean tuna which is beautifully complemented by this light and tangy dressing. The cooking time of the tuna will depend on the thickness of the steak.

LIME, MIRIN AND TAMARI DRESSING

finely grated rind and juice of 2 limes

1 tsp fresh ginger purée

2 tbsp honey

4 tbsp tamari soy sauce

300 g daikon (white radish)

2 medium carrots

1 yellow courgette

2 tbsp olive oil

4 tuna steaks

2 tbsp finely chopped mint

1 tsp black sesame seeds

NUTRITIONAL VALUES

1. To make the dressing, whisk the lime juice and rind, ginger purée, honey and tamari soy sauce together until evenly combined.

2. Peel the daikon and carrots. Shred the daikon, carrots and courgette into long, spaghetti-like strips using a mandoline, food processor attachment or sharp knife. Blanch in a pan of boiling water for 2 minutes or until starting to soften.

3. Heat the oil in a heavy frying pan and, when very hot, add the tuna steaks and cook for 1-2 minutes each side or until done to your liking.

4. Drain the vegetables and toss with half the mint and the sesame seeds. Divide among serving plates and top with the tuna steaks. Spoon the dressing over the steaks and serve garnished with the reserved mint.

CHINESE BAKED SALMON

SERVES **4-6**

The Chinese usually serve a whole fish at their New Year's banquets, but the dish can be enjoyed all year round – the spicing adds extra flavour to the salmon.

1 small whole salmon, or a large piece of salmon, weighing about 1.2 kg
8 spring onions, trimmed and finely sliced
5 cm piece ginger root, peeled and finely chopped
1-2 red chillies, seeded and finely chopped
light soy sauce
50 ml sesame oil

1 Preheat the oven to 220°C/gas mark 7. Lightly oil a large sheet of heavy foil, big enough to enclose the salmon, and place it on a lipped baking sheet.

2 Trim the salmon and slash the flesh deeply three times on each side – this helps the fish to cook more quickly. Place the fish on the foil and insert half the spring onions, all the ginger and the chillies into the cavity – press a little of the fish, then wrap it loosely in the foil. Bake in the hot oven for about 30 minutes, until the flesh offers no resistance when pierced with the tip of a sharp knife. Take care not to overcook the salmon or it will be dry.

3 Divide the salmon into portions and scatter the remaining spring onions among them. Meanwhile, heat the sesame oil in a small pan, then pour it over the salmon just before serving.

NUTRITIONAL VALUES

SALMON AND WILD MUSHROOM KEBABS

SERVES **4**

Thread chunky vegetables between the fish, such as courgettes, small tomatoes and onions to make a different version of these delicious kebabs.

1 kg salmon fillet or steaks, skinned
8 wild mushrooms, cleaned
1 small yellow pepper, cubed
freshly ground black pepper
juice and zest of 1 medium lime
1 garlic clove, peeled and crushed
1 tbsp garlic wine vinegar
2 tbsp olive oil
1 tsp prepared Dijon mustard
1 tbsp fresh dill, chopped
150 ml fish stock
lime wedges and fresh dill, to garnish
green salad, to serve

1. Wash the fish under running water and pat dry. Cut into cubes, removing any bones if using steaks. Halve the mushrooms and transfer to a shallow glass dish with the fish and yellow pepper. Season well.

2. Mix the lime juice and zest, garlic, vinegar, olive oil, mustard and dill. Pour into the glass dish to coat the ingredients well. Cover and marinate for 2 hours, turning occasionally.

3. Cut four wooden skewers in half. Thread on the fish, pepper and mushrooms, alternating ingredients. Reserve marinade.

4. Bring the water in the base of the steamer to the boil. Lay a sheet of foil in the base of the top of the steamer and arrange the kebabs inside. Cover with a tight-fitting lid and reduce heat slightly. Cook for 15 minutes.

5. Meanwhile, bring the marinade and stock to the boil in a saucepan until reduced by half. Arrange kebabs on a serving plate and pour the hot marinade over the top. Garnish with lime wedges and dill, and serve with green salad.

NUTRITIONAL VALUES

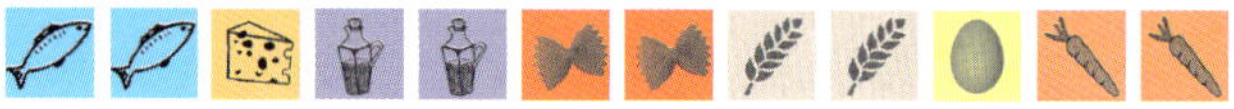

SEAFOOD GUMBO WITH OKRA

SERVES **8**

Okra is used as the thickener, so this gumbo is lighter than a roux-based gumbo. It is only mildly spicy. Use at least three different types of fish and shellfish, in whatever combination of fresh seafood is available: prawns, crab, oysters, frogs' legs, crayfish tails, clams, mussels, scallops, or filleted redfish, red snapper, cod or other fish, cut into cubes.

2 tbsp olive oil
450 g onions, chopped
2 large green peppers, chopped
2 celery stalks, chopped
3 garlic cloves, finely chopped
3 large or 4 medium tomatoes, seeded and chopped
225 g tin tomato sauce
1.75 litre fish stock
1 tbsp freshly squeezed lemon juice
2 bay leaves
1 tbsp fresh thyme or 1 tsp dried
1 tsp salt substitute (see page 12)
1/4 tsp black pepper
large pinch white pepper
1/2 tsp paprika
700 g okra, thawed and well drained if frozen, sliced
900 g mixed seafood
450 g cooked brown rice to serve
filé powder (optional)

1 In a large frying pan, heat the oil. Sauté the onion, pepper, celery and garlic until limp, about 5 minutes. Transfer to a large saucepan or stockpot and add the tomatoes, tomato sauce, fish stock, lemon juice and simmer, uncovered, for 5 minutes.

2 Add the okra and return to the boil, then reduce the heat and simmer for 30 minutes. Add the seafood: cubed fish and frogs' legs take the longest times to cook, oysters the least.

3 Spoon the rice into individual large bowls. Ladle the gumbo over the rice. If desired, add a pinch of filé powder to each bowl.

NUTRITIONAL VALUES

FISH PROVENÇAL

SERVES **4**

When cooking fish in a slow cooker it is best to skin it first. Slip a long sharp knife under the skin at the tail end, then slip it down the length of the fish or, if the fish is firm fleshed, rip the skin off.

- 4 cod or other firm white fish fillets weighing about 550 g
- 1 onion, peeled and sliced
- 1 yellow pepper, deseeded and sliced
- 425 g tin artichoke hearts, drained and cut in half
- 4 firm tomatoes, sliced
- 50 g pitted black olives
- 1 bay leaf
- salt substitute (see page 12)
- freshly ground black pepper
- 120 ml medium dry white wine
- snipped fresh chives, to garnish
- warm crusty bread or new potatoes and salad, to serve

1 Preheat the slow cooker on high. Skin the fish if necessary, cut into bite-sized pieces and place in the cooking pot. Add the remaining ingredients except for the wine and chives. Bring the wine to just below boiling point, pour over the fish, then cover with the lid.

2 Reduce the temperature to low and cook for 3-4 hours. Serve garnished with chives and with either warm crusty bread or new potatoes and salad.

NUTRITIONAL VALUES

DESSERTS

SLICED EXOTIC FRUITS WITH DATES

SERVES **6**

Almost any seasonal fruits are delicious sliced or cut up together in their natural juices or with a fruit purée.

- 1 Ogen melon, seeded and sliced in thin wedges and peeled
- 3 sweet seedless oranges, peeled and segmented, juice reserved
- 1 mango, peeled and thinly sliced
- 24 fresh lychees, peeled, or 1 425 g tin lychees in their own juice
- 12 Medjool dates, cut in half lengthways and stoned
- 1 pomegranate, cut in half, seeds reserved (optional)
- fresh mint leaves for garnish

1 Arrange slices of melon on each of the six individual plates in a fan shape. Arrange peeled orange segments and mango slices in an attractive pattern over the melon slices.

2 Evenly distribute fresh or tinned lychees over fruit and sprinkle on some reserved juices from all fruits.

3 Arrange four date halves on each plate and sprinkle over the pomegranate seeds, if using. Garnish with fresh mint leaves and serve.

NUTRITIONAL VALUES

MANGO MALAI

SERVES **4**

Traditionally you use double cream in Mango Malai, but by substituting low-fat yoghurt you reduce the amount of calories and still have a wonderfully refreshing dessert.

If you choose to use tinned mango instead, the finished desserts will contain 40 more calories, or 10 more calories per portion.

225 g fresh mango, flesh only

225 g low-fat natural yoghurt

2–3 tbsp artificial sugar

2 tsp lemon juice

pinch of nutmeg

50 g black grapes

1 Put the mango, yoghurt, sugar, lemon juice and nutmeg into a blender and process it until it is smooth.

2 Spoon the mixture into four serving dishes. Halve the grapes, discarding the pips, if any, and decorate the dessert with them. Serve chilled.

NUTRITIONAL VALUES

RHUBARB CRUMBLE WITH OATY TOPPING

SERVES **4**

Family members who like old-fashioned nursery puddings will love this sticky-toffee fruit layer topped with a healthy and delicious crumble oat mixture.

450 g rhubarb, trimmed and cut into 2.5 cm lengths
grated rind and juice of 1 orange
1 tbsp water
50 g stoned dates, chopped
2 tbsp clear honey
75 g wholewheat breadcrumbs
75 g rolled porridge oats
60 g polyunsaturated margarine, melted
50 g light muscovado sugar

1 Set the oven to 180°C/gas mark 4. Place the rhubarb, orange juice and rind, water, dates and honey in a 1 litre oven-proof dish.

2 For the topping, mix together the breadcrumbs, oats, margarine and sugar and spread the topping over the fruit. Bake in the oven for about 35 minutes, until the topping is golden. Serve piping hot.

NUTRITIONAL VALUES

MELON ICE

SERVES **4**

Any melon is suitable for the recipe. Incredibly colourful and refreshing, it is the perfect light end to any meal.

115 g sugar

3 mint sprigs

450 g melon, such as cantaloupe, galia or watermelon, seeded and diced

mint to decorate

NUTRITIONAL VALUES

1 Set the freezer to rapid freeze. Place the sugar in a pan with 125 ml water. Add the mint and cook over a gentle heat until the sugar dissolves. Remove the pan from the heat and strain the syrup. Discard the mint sprigs. Stir in 300 ml cold water.

2 Place the melon in a food processor and purée for 30 seconds until smooth. Stir into the syrup. Mix well and cool. Place the mixture in a freezerproof container and freeze for 1 hour.

3 Remove from the freezer and pour the melon mixture into a bowl and whisk until smooth. Return to a clean freezer-proof container and freeze for a further 30 minutes. Repeat the whisking process every 30 minutes for $2\frac{1}{2}$ hours. Scoop into dishes, decorate with mint, and serve immediately.

FRUIT SALAD

SERVES **4**

Getting a good portion of fruit each day has great health benefits. And having a fruit as a dessert is a delicious way of increasing your fruit intake.

2 medium-sized juicy oranges
2 limes
30 g raspberries
30 g strawberries
30 g blueberries
30 g blackberries
1 large papaya
2 kiwi fruit, peeled and sliced
20 g fresh coconut meat, shredded, or 25 g desiccated coconut

1 With a sharp paring knife, remove all the skin from the oranges. Holding the oranges over a medium bowl to catch juices, cut along the membranes of the oranges so the segments fall into the bowl as well. Repeat the process for the limes.

2 Add raspberries, strawberries, blueberries and blackberries. Cover and refrigerate for 2 hours.

3 Peel papaya, cut in half and remove the seeds. Cut each half into 1 cm slices and arrange on four plates with sliced kiwi fruit.

4 Spoon berry and orange mixture, with juices, over papaya. Sprinkle with coconut.

NUTRITIONAL VALUES

HONEYDEW MELON

SERVES **4**

If you think of melon as a watery nothingness, think again. In this recipe we use crème de menthe to bring out the flavour of the melon; you could also try Midori, the melon liqueur. Serve with balls of watermelon, to provide an exciting colour contrast, and the crisp biscuits known as langue du chat.

125 g caster sugar

350 ml water

1 tbsp lemon juice

1 small honeydew melon (about 675 g)

1 large egg white

1–1 1/2 tbsp crème de menthe

mint leaves to decorate

1 Dissolve the sugar slowly in the water; bring to the boil, then simmer the syrup for 5 minutes. Add the lemon juice after boiling. Remove the pan from the heat and leave until completely cool.

2 Blend the melon to a smooth purée in a liquidizer or a food processor, then blend in the cooled sugar syrup. Whisk the egg white until soft and frothy, then fold in the melon mixture with crème de menthe to taste.

3 Turn into an ice-cream machine, then freeze-churn until ready to serve. Decorate with mint leaves.

NUTRITIONAL VALUES

CHOCOLATE-DIPPED STRAWBERRIES

SERVES **2**

A sophisticated yet very simple dessert. Fabulous for dinner parties or a great way to indulge yourself.

125 g plain chocolate
6 strawberries

1 Melt the chocolate in a double boiler.

2 Holding the strawberries by the stalk, dip each one in the melted chocolate until evenly covered. Place on a greaseproof paper and refrigerate.

NUTRITIONAL VALUES

NECTARINE YOGHURT ICE

SERVES **2**

The sweet freshness of nectarines blends well with the flavour and texture of yoghurt to give a light, refreshing ice. A perfect ice for serving with rhubarb tart or plum compôte.

200 g roughly puréed nectarines
about 4 medium fruits
1 tbsp lemon juice
100 g caster sugar
575 g low-fat natural yoghurt

1 Beat all the ingredients together until smooth. Spoon into an ice-cream machine, then freeze-churn until ready to serve.

NUTRITIONAL VALUES

LOW FAT OAT AND ORANGE BISCUITS

MAKES **20**

These little biscuits are hard to resist. Rolled in oatmeal, they are crisp on the outside, and soft in the centre with a mild orange flavour.

3 tbsp polyunsaturated margarine
60 g granulated brown sugar
1 egg white, lightly beaten
2 tbsp skimmed milk
3 tbsp raisins
grated rind of 1 orange
150 g self-raising flour
90 g oatmeal
strips of orange rind to decorate

NUTRITIONAL VALUES

1 Preheat the oven to 180°C/gas mark 4. Cream the margarine and suger together until the mixture is light and fluffy. Add the egg white, milk, raisins and orange rind. Fold in the flour and bring the mixture together to form a dough, then roll into 20 equal-sized balls.

2 Place the oatmeal in a shallow bowl, roll each dough ball in the oatmeal to coat completely, pressing gently. Place the biscuits on non-stick baking sheets, spacing well apart. Flatten each round slightly.

3 Bake for 15 minutes or until they are golden. Cool on a wire rack, then decorate the biscuits. Store in airtight containers.

RAISIN AND HONEY BREAD

MAKES **1 LOAF**

This loaf contains a high proportion of yoghurt which gives it a white, light centre.

NUTRITIONAL VALUES

300 g plain flour

1 1/2 tsp baking powder

1/2 tsp bicarbonate of soda

1/2 tsp salt substitute (see page 12)

300 ml plain yoghurt

2 egg whites

55 g raisins

2 tbsp honey

butter for greasing

1. Preheat the oven to 220°C/gas mark 7. Mix the flour, baking powder, bicarbonate of soda and salt in a large bowl. Whisk together the yoghurt and egg whites and fold into the flour mixture with the rasins and honey.

2. Grease a large loaf tin and spoon in the mixture. Bake for 20 minutes until golden. Cool slightly and turn out of the tin. Serve warm.

INDEX